Andrei Sakharov

HOOVER
INSTITUTION
STANFORD
UNIVERSITY

The Hoover Institution gratefully acknowledges
the following individuals and foundations
for their significant support to the project
that led to this publication:

THOMAS AND BARBARA STEPHENSON

THE WILLIAM AND FLORA HEWLETT FOUNDATION

PRESTON AND CAROLYN BUTCHER

JOHN AND ANN DOERR

FLORA FAMILY FOUNDATION

THE KORET FOUNDATION

THE MARY JO AND DICK KOVACEVICH FAMILY FOUNDATION

WILLIAM AND SUSAN OBERNDORF

PAUL AND SANDRA OTELLINI

THE THOMAS AND STACEY SIEBEL FOUNDATION

Andrei Sakharov

The Conscience of Humanity

Edited by
Sidney D. Drell and George P. Shultz

HOOVER INSTITUTION PRESS
STANFORD UNIVERSITY   STANFORD, CALIFORNIA

www.hoover.org

Hoover Institution Press Publication No. 663

Hoover Institution at Leland Stanford Junior University, Stanford, California 94305-6003

First printing 2014
21 20 19 18 17 16 15   7 6 5 4 3 2 1

Manufactured in the United States of America

The paper used in this publication meets the minimum Requirements of the American National Standard for Information Sciences—Permanence of Paper for Printed Library Materials, ANSI/NISO Z39.48-1992. ⊗

Cataloging-in-Publication Data is available from the Library of Congress.
ISBN: 978-0-8179-1895-8 (pbk. : alk. paper)
ISBN: 978-0-8179-1896-5 (epub)
ISBN: 978-0-8179-1897-2 (mobi)
ISBN: 978-0-8179-1898-9 (PDF)

Contents

     David Holloway

11   A Global Commons: A Vision Whose Time Has Come   131
     James E. Goodby

     Conference Agenda   143

     About the Participants   147

     Index   155

Preface

Sidney D. Drell, Jim Hoagland, and George P. Shultz

Science and technology have dramatically reshaped global com-munication, finance, and culture in the three decades that have elapsed since Mikhail Gorbachev gained power in the Kremlin in 1985 and, working together with Ronald Reagan, began to bring the Cold War to an end. But the vision of a generally peaceful world that the end of the Cold War offered is now dimmed by a series of dangerous and destructive confrontations. Historians may come to call the era through which we have just lived the Thirty Years' Interregnum.

Deadly new civil conflicts and international terrorism wreak growing havoc on global stability and on the human condi-tion itself. Repressive governments *and* armed non-state orga-nizations—often waving the banners of religion—inflict savage human rights abuses on civilian populations and have helped create the greatest flows of refugees seen since World War II. Governments again seek to preserve waning powers and secu-rity rather than continue to expand economic and social progress internationally. Cross-border aggression in Europe, bloody sec-tarian conflict throughout the Middle East and Africa, and big-power tensions in Asia are the engines of change in 2015, not the technologically inspired spread of ideas and goods that marked the first decades of modern globalization.

In this changed setting, a fundamental grim reality of the Cold War endures: mankind still possesses the knowledge and means to destroy itself with nuclear weapons—a power that is no longer under the sole, firm control of two military extended alliances committed to maintaining their own versions of the status quo.

Andrei Sakharov, Stanford University, 1989. Photo by
Harvey Lynch.

To gain a deeper understanding of how these emerging challenges interact with and intensify the nuclear menace, Stanford
University's Hoover Institution convened a conference focused
on the life and principles of Andrei Sakharov, the eminent Russian
nuclear physicist and courageous human rights campaigner who
was awarded the Nobel Peace Prize in 1975 and is often described
as a spokesman for the conscience of humanity. We believe his
work and thinking can serve as fixed reference points for an effort
to find solutions that must also emerge on a global scale.

The conference of scholars, historians, military commanders,
theologians, scientists, technological entrepreneurs, opinion-
makers, and others began fittingly on World Human Rights Day,
December 10, 2014. Sakharov had demonstrated an unflinch-
ing courage to speak out in circumstances of great personal danger—to tell truth to power with dignity and consistency, and to

demand openness and truth from rulers. Without truth and the freedom to express it, he maintained, people lacked the power to be free.

The conference also began four days before the twenty-fifth anniversary of Sakharov's death in 1989. His extraordinary life saw him go from playing the leading role in designing and building the most powerful thermonuclear weapon ever exploded (the so-called hydrogen bomb) to demanding an end to the testing of such weapons and their eventual elimination. His early awareness of the environmental damage inflicted by nuclear testing echoes through our current debates on the state of the world and its physical well-being. And the refusal of the leading Soviet politicians of the day to heed his warnings about the damage being done to the world's environment led directly to Sakharov's unfaltering opposition to totalitarian control wherever it existed. The metamorphosis of Sakharov—from a distinguished physical scientist repeatedly honored by his government into a courageous, outspoken dissident who devoted himself to voicing his humanitarian convictions, his compassion for the persecuted, and his devotion to the freedom of the human spirit—forms a compelling story that this book tells.

The essays that follow establish that Sakharov was passionate about human rights and dissent in ways that link him to Nelson Mandela, Martin Luther King Jr., Lech Walesa, Vaclav Havel, Wei Jingsheng, Fang Lizhi, Aung San Suu Kyi, Oswaldo Payá Sardiñas, and others who fought to advance human rights by focusing the world media on their struggle. They too were passionate advocates, uniformly and unmistakably determined, self-aware, and certain that their beliefs in human rights would eventually prevail. In that sense, they became political prophets. But their motivation also seemed personal, as it was for Sakharov: dissent practiced in a closed, highly propagandized system is a form of sanity, a way to cling to reason in an irrational and arbitrary world of forces that deal with the citizen not only unfairly but inhumanely.

In his essay (chapter 1), Serge Schmemann examines both the international image that Sakharov created through his appeal to the conscience of mankind and the reality behind it: "As his activism gathered pace, he was often perceived by the outside world as a Russian Don Quixote, a tousled, retiring intellectual who had built a doomsday weapon and was now tilting at the windmills of an all-powerful state.

"But his friends saw a different Sakharov—a brilliant, profound, and courageous thinker who, in his purity of vision, posed a fundamental challenge to the state simply by calling *evil* by its name and demanding that the state abide by its own laws." Sakharov and his indomitable wife, Elena Bonner, became a clearinghouse of information for the world's journalists on Soviet abuses of rights. "His power was in his example," Schmemann writes.

Sakharov, in particular, spoke directly to the multidimensional future that he helped bring into being and glimpsed with remarkable clarity. He was a theoretical physicist, but the relationship between technology and broader social and political purposes was central to his life and work, a point made by David Holloway in chapter 10, "Moral Reasoning and Practical Purpose." Sakharov was a scientist, a patriot, and a humanist in the broadest sense of those words. He gave a sense of this in writing these words in the magazine *Physics Today* in 1981: "Because of the international nature of our profession, scientists form the one real worldwide community which exists today." He appealed first to his scientific colleagues abroad, and then to mankind at large, for solidarity in resolving the growing threats to human survival—some of which stemmed from science and technology.

In 1974, Sakharov presciently forecast a universal information system (UIS) "which will give everyone access at any given moment to the contents of any book that has ever been published or any magazine or any fact."[1] This statement was written before the advent of the personal computer, the Internet, or cell phones, as Christopher Stubbs notes in chapter 7, "The Sakharov Conditions, Disruptive Technologies, and Human Rights."

Sakharov's metamorphosis is rooted in his keen awareness that the great benefits that science and technology deliver are often accompanied by incalculable risks that become apparent only later. People everywhere today, with little effort, can find out what is going on, can communicate with each other on cell phones or computers, and organize. But ancient group hatreds and prejudices take deeper root and flourish through the communications revolution he foresaw. Furthermore, Sakharov asked whether—in an information technology-connected world with a UIS—individual citizens would strengthen their moral compasses or, instead, society would become too responsive to the voices of others and individuals would be less willing to take principled stands. Globalization sparks atavistic fears and fundamentalist backlashes that have begun to call into question the viability of the modern state system that grew out of Europe's Thirty Years' War.

Diversity is in fact everywhere in this information and communications age and it must be recognized for the good, and less good, it produces. It contributes to the accelerating fragmentation of the world's bodies politic, shredding confidence in the abilities and good faith of the world's political leaders, titans of industry, banking executives, and other authority figures. Worse, many of these leaders feed the loss of faith by systematically refusing, in this era of greater transparency and visibility, to take responsibility either for their own contributions to the turmoil or for their inadequacy in confronting it. Political marketing has replaced political dialogue and political accountability in many countries.

The failure of many of the world's leading newspapers and media empires to understand this fragmentation undermined their business models and their legitimacy, further deepening the public's confusion about authority and reliability. Increasingly, dissidents must establish their own direct communications networks, braving the state's ability to use technology to track and punish them.

Sakharov's fate helps us understand how much has, and has not, changed. Dictators everywhere fear that dissent is a communicable "evil," like disease, and they try to quarantine it immediately. Thus the Soviet leadership stripped Sakharov of three Hero of Socialist Labor medals and forced him into internal exile in the closed city of Gorky in 1980 to keep him from communicating directly for more than six years with his fellow citizens in Russia, foreign dissidents, and journalists. But he continued to communicate his ideas through letters and statements made available to others. The eleven essays in this book, prepared for this conference and subsequently edited, illuminate this fierce resistance to official persecution, which inspired political rebels in the Soviet Union and Eastern Europe to chip away at the Iron Curtain and Soviet repression until Gorbachev freed Sakharov from internal exile and ultimately freed tens of millions more from repression. Today, the first response to mass protests in Hong Kong or Cairo is to try to shut down the Internet and silence dissent, just as the Kremlin tried to do with Sakharov.

The roots of Sakharov's insistence on integrity and accountability lie deep in his intensely Russian family life and his training to become a scientist—politically "the ultimate insider," as Professor J. Bryan Hehir qualifies the profession in chapter 2, "The Scientist as Prophet: Sakharov's World and Ours"—who then becomes the prophet of human rights and justice, or the ultimate political outsider.

Sakharov was a product of his times. For Sakharov as a young man, as for most Soviet citizens at the time, World War II had been an elemental struggle for survival. A sense of collective sacrifice and heroic struggle was a recurring theme in Sakharov's thinking as he made crucial contributions to understanding nuclear fusion in its practical applications to civilian power (the Tokamak design) and to the design and construction of thermonuclear super-bombs, the so-called hydrogen bombs that explode with thousands of times the destructive energy released by the relatively primitive devices that obliterated Hiroshima and Nagasaki.

Unjust imprisonment and other crimes committed by Stalin and the Soviet system were subordinated to the national sense that the times required suffering and sacrifice. That applied to the awe-inspiring super-bomb Sakharov was developing. The Right Reverend William Swing's essay, "The Soul and Sakharov," chapter 3, quotes a key passage from Sakharov on his work to reach parity with the United States, which had already tested thermonuclear weapons: "What was the most important for me at the time . . . was the conviction that our work was essential. . . . I understood, of course, the terrifying, inhuman nature of the weapons we were building. But the recent war had also been an exercise in barbarity; and . . . I regarded myself as a soldier in this new scientific war . . . the sacrifices that our country has made should not be in vain. . . . We never questioned the vital importance of our work."

Sakharov had not participated in the Soviet program to develop first-generation atomic bombs, which the Soviets first tested in 1949. But he entered the project to build the super-bomb enthusiastically. That is, he insisted on the necessity of strategic parity for progress in controlling nuclear weapons and the arms race, and for eventually achieving the long-term goal of disarmament. For him, it was a way forward to assure peace and security for his people.

During his first visit to the United States, in December 1988, Sakharov observed: "In the United States, independently, the same kind of work was being carried out. The American scientists in their work were guided by the same feelings of this work being vital for the interests of the country. But, while both sides felt that this kind of work was vital to maintain balance, I think that what we were doing at that time was a great tragedy. It was a tragedy that reflected the tragic state of the world that made it necessary, in order to maintain peace, to do such terrible things. We will never know whether it was really true that our work contributed at some period of time toward maintaining peace in the world but, at least at the time we were doing it, we were convinced this was the case."

Sakharov's journey into dissent was not one he made alone. Other scientists instrumental in creating nuclear weapons also were among the first to understand the terrible risks they had created, and to try to mitigate them. In 1950, one year after the Soviet Union tested its first atomic bomb (a single-stage device like the Nagasaki bomb), the United States made a fateful decision to develop and test a two-stage thermonuclear weapon that would become known as the hydrogen bomb. President Truman, faced with a highly charged military and strategic confrontation with the Soviet Union, rejected the recommendation of scientists on the General Advisory Committee to the US Atomic Energy Commission that "enough [information] be declassified about the super bomb so that a public statement of policy can be made at this time." But Truman did not opt for public debate, and proceeded with the hydrogen bomb.

Two of the great pioneer nuclear physicists and participants in the US nuclear effort, Enrico Fermi and I. I. Rabi, wrote in their personal addendum to the GAC report: "It is clear that the use of such a weapon cannot be justified on any ethical ground which gives a human being a certain individuality and dignity even if he happens to be a resident of an enemy country."

As Sakharov developed a growing concern about the harmful health effects due to nuclear radiation resulting from atmospheric nuclear testing of the high-yield thermonuclear bombs he and his Western counterparts were creating, he also developed passionate opposition to the Soviet Union's continuing abuses of human rights. This led to his public appeals in 1966 for the liberation of victims of repression who were being incarcerated, some in psychiatric care institutions or gulag camps.

Religion seems to have played no direct role in Sakharov's transition from a scientific warrior to a courageous fighter for human rights. Although he grew up in a family with a deeply religious grandmother, as a teenager he rejected God. Later he commented that, with the death of his grandmother when he was twenty years old, "soul" departed from the Sakharov house. However, he clearly was a man who exercised strong moral judgment in his actions as well as his writings as he addressed important challenges facing the world.

Sakharov had a clear and compelling moral compass to guide him as he navigated the strong countervailing tides of political policy and scientific reality. As the Soviet Union approached technical nuclear parity with the United States, he found that his government rejected scientific advice to temper the program to avoid growing damage to the environment and the health of human beings from radioactive fallout. In his essay, David Holloway describes Sakharov's extensive personal efforts, including the

...tion (with Nikita Khrushchev's permission) of an article ...entific journal[2] concerning the potential harmful biological ... of explosive testing in the atmosphere. His detailed tech- ...proposal to reorganize the Soviet program so that it could ...ed without requiring nuclear test explosions was rejected ...y Khrushchev after a short unilateral testing moratorium by the Soviet Union. The Soviets resumed testing until they agreed to a one-year moratorium, starting near the end of 1958, together with the United States and the United Kingdom.

In fact, these three countries enforced a moratorium on all nuclear explosive testing for three years, until 1961. When Sakharov received word in 1961 that the Soviet government was planning to renew testing, he wrote a letter to Khrushchev opposing such a step. In an angry rebuff, Khrushchev wrote, "Leave politics to us—we're the specialists. You make your bombs and test them, and we won't interfere with you; we'll help you. But remember, we have to conduct our policies from a position of strength."

The Soviets' concern was that they were far behind the American program in testing and starting to deploy thermonuclear weapons designed to release multi-megatons of destructive energy. Sakharov was concerned by the growing evidence that performing such tests above ground was producing significant amounts of radioactivity in the atmosphere, which was harmful to human beings. He chose to continue his weapons work while seeking to persuade Soviet leaders to accept an American proposal to ban all above-ground explosive testing. This would be an important step toward an eventual comprehensive test ban treaty, once it was agreed that compliance with such a treaty could be verified. The outcome of this effort, which drew Sakharov's strongly expressed support, was a Limited Test Ban Treaty (LTBT) banning nuclear weapons tests "or any other nuclear explosions" in the atmosphere, in outer space, and under water, signed and ratified in 1963 by Great Britain, the Soviet Union, and the United States.

The Soviet Union's insistence on continuing very-large-yield atmospheric tests (also being carried out by the United States) before the LTBT entered into force on October 10, 1963, was a major factor in Sakharov's total and public rupture with the Kremlin, which responded by removing him from the nuclear program in 1968. This episode heightened Sakharov's awareness of, and sensitivity to, excessive and expanding restrictions by Moscow on human rights, including—in particular—free speech.

The strength of his commitment to the importance of "disarmament talks, which offer a ray of hope in the dark world of suicidal nuclear madness," is evident in his statement in 1981, during the first year of his exile in Gorky. "Despite all that has happened, I feel that the questions of war and peace and disarmament are so crucial that they must be given absolute priority even in the most difficult circumstances. It is imperative that all possible means be used to solve these questions and to lay the groundwork for further progress. Most urgent of all are steps to avert a nuclear war, which is the greatest peril confronting the modern world. The goals of all responsible people in the world coincide in this regard, including, I hope and believe, the Soviet leaders. . . ." To further emphasize his conviction of the critical importance of an open democratic society with freedom of information, freedom of conscience, and the right to publish, he insisted, "Without a resolution of political and humanitarian problems, progress in disarmament and international security will be extremely difficult, if not impossible."

Sakharov persisted with protests and hunger strikes even when prospects for improving the Soviet Union's oppressive system were very dim. His description of those days made him a commanding beacon for all dissidents, then and now: "There is a need to create ideals even when you can't see any route by which to achieve them, because if there are no ideals, then there can be no hope and then one would be completely in the dark, in a hopeless blind alley." He also cautioned that only progress in establishing open democratic societies with freedom of information, freedom of conscience, and the right to publish could bring progress in averting nuclear war, to him the greatest peril confronting the modern world.

The urgency of strengthening and protecting human freedom has not lessened in today's world. Nuclear deterrence based on maintaining excessively large nuclear arsenals remains an existential danger as its effectiveness is challenged by the spread of nuclear technology and the ability and interest of more countries to acquire nuclear weapons. Furthermore, as we have previously noted, irrepressible progress in science and technology is introducing unexpected challenges to today's society by creating new means to effect major changes, not all of which will be beneficial.

Spurred by failures in governing in an age of diversity, deadly attacks on humanity by apocalyptic non-state terrorists are occurring with greater frequency throughout the world. Regimes ignore—or, in places like Bashar Assad's Syria or the jihadist "caliphate" of the Islamic State, bloodily repress—the growing diversity of ideas, peoples, lifestyles, and patterns of economic activity enriching societies agile enough to adapt to modernizing diversity. The specter of such groups gaining access to nuclear weapons is almost too horrible to contemplate.

Russia's assault on Ukraine unmistakably seeks to return Europe to a time of "spheres of influence," whether or not it leads to a total return to the Cold War conditions Gorbachev and his partners managed to marginalize for three decades. Vladimir Putin's deliberately deceptive diplomacy and covert state action smack of Soviet practices.

The disappearance of the Soviet Union has not meant an absence of battlefields. For more than three decades, the United States has been episodically involved in combat in the Middle East. There and elsewhere, American and European governments have felt morally impelled to intervene on humanitarian grounds and to prevent genocide. The extreme duress of the battlefield poses the most difficult challenge to remaining true to our moral and ethical principles. A strong message that emerged from our discussions was the critical importance of strong, clear—and ethical—military leadership in developing a national strategy and in conducting operations. Drawing on the examples set by Andrei Sakharov in the realm of science and politics, both Admiral James O. Ellis Jr. (US Navy, Ret.) in "New Dilemmas in Ethics, Technology, and War: Sakharov's Principles in Today's World" (chapter 8) and General James N. Mattis (US Marine

Corps, Ret.) in "A Military Perspective" (chapter 9) emphasize the importance of developing strategies and conducting operations consistent with the principles of our nation's Founding Fathers. As Mattis writes: "One of our military's lessons learned (or re-learned) over this last decade of war is that we must integrate and use *all* our national power in defense of freedom. By 'all' we must include our moral power: we should never surrender the moral high ground, whether in policy or military orders."

As discussed by James Goodby in chapter 11, "A Global Commons: A Vision Whose Time Has Come," progress in such an effort will require nothing less than creating a global commons; i.e., creating institutions that can deal with such threats to all humanity. He quotes this warning from Sakharov: "The division of mankind threatens it with destruction . . . any action increasing the division of mankind, any preaching of the incompatibility of world ideologies and nations is madness and a crime." Goodby goes on to argue that "changes in the international system require power-sharing by governments with regions, global institutions, major urban centers, and economic organizations with global reach . . ."

In the December 2014 conference, we explored four scientific areas where major changes are in progress that are already having important societal impacts. Christopher Stubbs's discussion in chapter 7 of Sakharov's foresight on the creation of a universal information system leads into an examination of the impact of such disruptive technology on social equilibrium and governance. This is emphasized in this quote by Sakharov in Stubbs's essay: "Even the partial realization of the UIS will profoundly affect every person, his leisure activities, and his intellectual and artistic development. Unlike television . . . the UIS will give each person maximum freedom of choice and will require individual activity. But the true historic role of the UIS will be to break down the barriers to the exchange of information among countries and people."[3]

Throughout the years of the US-Soviet Cold War, the threat of a nuclear holocaust was a major concern. It was recognized, based on sophisticated calculations, that a large-scale nuclear war in which approximately one thousand megatons were detonated would cause many hundreds of millions of casualties and the end of our civilization, if not of the human species itself. (A megaton is the equivalent of the energy released by a million tons of TNT.) It would also significantly modify the global atmosphere, leading to a nuclear winter (i.e., worldwide cooling). The principal cause for this phenomenon would be the large quantities of soot that would be lofted into the atmosphere. Soot, which has the optical properties of carbon without organic compounds, is generated by wood fires such as were created by intense bombing in several cities in World War II. What is new in recent analyses, as discussed in chapter 4, "Environmental Effects of Nuclear War" by Raymond Jeanloz, is that enough soot would be lofted in a very limited regional war (with the detonation of one hundred Hiroshima-scale fifteen-kiloton nuclear bombs, or close to one-thousandth of a major one) to cause serious societal consequences. For example, preliminary calculations suggest that food supplies would be greatly reduced because of shorter growing seasons and harsher weather conditions lasting for several years. More analysis is needed and is in progress on how all levels of nuclear war would affect the environment.

But the implications are clear: nuclear weapons technology is proliferating, new countries are engaged in ongoing efforts to acquire nuclear weapons, and our current policy of nuclear deterrence based on maintaining a capability of massive assured destruction is ineffective against apocalyptic terrorists. Therefore, we should renew efforts to create conditions of trust and transparency so that a world without nuclear weapons can be viewed as both desirable and technically practical in terms of verifying compliance.

The nuclear realm blasted open seventy years ago. A similar revolution is occurring in the sphere of bioscience today, as discussed by Lucy Shapiro in chapter 5, "Decoding the Biosphere and the Infectious Disease Threat." During the past twenty years, explosive progress has been made in scientists' ability to sequence the DNA double helix which contains the instructions used by every living cell to direct the business of life. This is true of all forms of life—not only humans, but also pathogens, including viruses, bacteria, and other microorganisms. They can be altered to protect our health or to unleash major life-threatening pandemics. Mankind can now engineer the genes encoded in DNA and change their function for better or worse. We can identify viruses for vaccine production, on one hand, or for their potential use as biological weapons on the other. Members of the scientific community—both those in the laboratory and those with policy responsibility in governments—face very difficult decisions on what, if any, regulations should be placed on research on dual-use pathogens and whether to impose delays versus open publication of findings. Similar concerns have been raised since the 1970s, when recombinant DNA technology was first published and first raised concerns about the potential use of genetically altered strains by bioterrorists and about the possibility that virulent pathogens could accidentally escape the labs, even those with the highest safety protocols.

Given the enormous increase in data-handling power and the precision in today's bioscience laboratories, including enduring unknowns in the ability to handle potential mutations in pathogens over time, facing up to such concerns remains a major challenge. Bioscience has joined nuclear weapons as one of the existential challenges to mankind, as Sakharov would surely have agreed.

On a more optimistic note—as discussed by Elizabeth Holmes in chapter 6, "Diagnosis, Reinvented for the Individual"—there are recent technical advances in medical diagnostics that promise major advances in one of the most basic human rights: enabling individuals to gain access to information about their own health, at greatly reduced and affordable costs. Furthermore, this information can be gained by testing well before diseases develop, enabling prevention before it is too late to do anything but treat them. The mobility, efficiency, and relative simplicity of advanced medical diagnostics also promise to be of great value in treating wounded soldiers on the battlefield, where time and proximity are so crucial. In all aspects, this is a good-news story about welcome progress toward developing a much more cost-effective and efficient global health care system.

Sakharov became heavily engaged in preserving and strengthening what he called in a 1974 essay "the human in human being." Among the requirements to achieve this goal he included "strengthening international trust, defense of human rights, justice, and freedom, deep social progress and democratization and the strengthening of the moral, spiritual side of a human being." Looking ahead, he expressed optimism that "mankind will find a solution to the complex problem of combining tremendous, necessary, inescapable technological progress with the preservation of the human in a human being and the natural in nature." But he also frequently reminded us of the unique danger of a nuclear war and the overriding importance of achieving a world free of nuclear weapons, emphasizing, "A large nuclear war would be a calamity of indescribable proportions and absolutely unpredictable consequences, with the uncertainties tending toward the worst . . ." and "Nuclear weapons only make sense as a means of deterring nuclear aggression by a potential enemy, i.e., a nuclear war cannot be planned with the aim of winning it. Nuclear weapons cannot be viewed as a means of restraining aggression carried out by means of conventional weapons."

Scientific research is an adventure of discovery by the human mind and, as such, is amoral. But practical applications of advances in science also have given mankind unprecedented powers to affect our lives, be it through genetic engineering, environmental change, or the creation of nuclear weapons of such enormous destructive energy that their use in war could mean the end of modern civilization, if not of the human species. This means that the scientific community also bears a special obligation to help guide society to understand the implications in making policy decisions about applying new technical advances.

We end with a fitting tribute to Andrei Sakharov by his friend, colleague, and long-persecuted dissident, Lev Kopelev,[4] who is widely recognized as the mathematician Rubin in Aleksandr Solzhenitsyn's book *The First Circle:*

And he suffered, he suffered the suffering of every man. I don't know if I can explain it, the soul of Sakharov who suffers for each suffering man. He loves his work, he loves his physics, he can't live without his physics. But when he got a phone call that some-one was arrested, or that someone had been searched, he got up and got a taxi or a trolley.

In his moving tribute after Sakharov's death, Kopelev wrote: "The majesty of his spirit, the power of his intellect, and the purity of his soul, his chivalrous courage and selfless kindness feed my faith in the future of Russia and mankind."

Notes

1. Andrei Sakharov, "Tomorrow: The View from Red Square," *Saturday Review of Literature*, August 24, 1974.
2. *Atomnaia Energiia* [Atomic energy], 1958.
3. Sakharov, "View from Red Square."
4. *The Guardian*, December 29, 1981.

Acknowledgments

The editors extend their deep appreciation to the many people associated with the Hoover Institution who planned and organized the 2014 conference "Andrei Sakharov and the Conscience of Humanity" and to those whose efforts led to the publication of this book.

We are indebted to the staff of the Hoover Institution Press. In particular, it was a pleasure to work with Barbara Arellano, managing editor; Elizabeth Berg, production editor; and Barbara Egbert, copy editor. Their professionalism was matched by their constructive approach to producing this book. We also thank Summer Tokash, Bonnie Rose, and Susan Southworth, who handled the many logistical details of the conference and the subsequent manuscript preparation.

Special thanks go to Linda Bernard and the staff of the Hoover Institution Archives, who assembled a fascinating trove of Sakharov material to display during the conference reception and dinner. We are also grateful to Harvey Lynch for allowing us to use several of his fine photographs of Andrei Sakharov.

Finally, the conference and this book would not have been possible without the generosity of Tom Stephenson and the Hewlett Foundation, which we acknowledge with great thanks.

The Evolution of Andrei Sakharov's Thinking

Serge Schmemann

December 14, 2014, was the twenty-fifth anniversary of Andrei Dmitrievich Sakharov's death. He holds an honored place in the pantheon of the world's greatest scientists, reformers, and champions of human rights.

I never personally met Sakharov—he was whisked off to internal exile in Gorky soon after I arrived, and returned to Moscow soon after I left. But I did get to know his wife, Elena Bonner, well, and through her, through their hunger strikes, through the dissident trials during my time in Moscow, and through the moral power that Sakharov continued to exert from his isolation in Gorky, he played a central role in my reporting.

Still, I find today that defining Sakharov's exact place in Soviet history is no easy task. As Sakharov himself said so often, "the truth is never simple." Neither is legacy.

Certainly there was no one like him in the dissident movement, no one who rose to such exalted heights and was so prepared to lose everything in support of human rights; nobody who had his combination of activism and modesty, boldness and shyness.

His very existence was something of a miracle. A descendant of priests and military officers, he was born to that genteel class of Russian intellectuals and professionals known as the intelligentsia, which through Russian history produced revolutionaries, poets, and scientists convinced that the most important thing was to do something useful.

Much of the old intelligentsia fled after the Russian Revolution. Many of those who survived were caught up in the purges; and if they survived that, there was the war.

Sakharov survived, and his genius found him a place in the machinery created by Joseph Stalin and Lavrenty Beria to assure Soviet military might. The state needed scientists, and the masters understood that science required not only coercion and threat, but also independence and intellectual freedom.

The solution was to seal the scientists in a gilded cage, isolate them in installations closed not only to foreigners but to most Soviet citizens, give them the highest level of privilege and equipment, and make clear that all this was conditional on producing what the state required.

Sakharov was a willing member of that system, convinced like so many scientists of the era that they were soldiers on the front lines of a global struggle which required sacrifice and suffering. He never repudiated or regretted creating a weapon of unimaginable power, believing that only a balance of power would prevent its use.

His embrace of human rights did not come through a sudden conversion. Scrupulously honest, and almost naïve in his understanding of politics and power, he came to it in stages. Let me give you a brief chronology of the metamorphosis.

First came his concern about the radioactive fallout from atmospheric testing. But in those years, in the 1950s, the concerns were still new, and raising them was possible within the scientific and political elite. These were issues Sakharov could take up directly with Nikita Khrushchev, even though he was at times rebuffed and put in his place for meddling in politics.

Then came the Academy of Science elections in 1964 at which Sakharov openly spoke out against accepting an ally of the pseudo-scientist Trofim Lysenko. The Academy of Science, in fact, was probably the closest to a democratic institution in the Soviet state, where full members could still vote to reject a candidate pushed by the Kremlin.

So far, Sakharov's activities were still within the bounds of permissible debate for someone of his standing in the elite. Yet as Sakharov noted in his *Memoirs*, the academy vote, like the struggle against atmospheric testing, marked another step on the way to becoming active in civic affairs.

The turning point for Sakharov, as for the entire dissident movement, came in the mid-1960s. These were years in which Sakharov signed a petition against the rehabilitation of Stalin, followed by a letter against the enactment of the law against defaming the Soviet state, which became the basis for the prosecution of many dissidents, followed by a decision to join in a demonstration on Pushkin Square on Constitution Day.

Then came his first letter, this one to Leonid Brezhnev, in support of a dissident, and then his involvement in the movement to save Lake Baikal.

What is amazing to realize now is that in those years, Sakharov had such high rank that he could pick up a special phone and directly call the KGB chief, Yuri Andropov, as he did in 1967 to seek the release of the writers Andrei Sinyavsky and Yuli Daniel.

These phones, known as *vertushka,* connected members of the top *nomenklatura* [chief officials]—I managed to steal one from the Kremlin during the chaos of 1991, and I learned then that the name, *vertushka,* which means "dial," comes from the fact that the elite network was the first to use dial phones.

On that call, Sakharov was told that Sinyavsky and Daniel would be released in a general amnesty, but they never were.

Step by step, Sakharov developed what he described as a growing compulsion to speak out on the fundamental issues of the age.

Finally, in 1968—that remarkable year of social rebellion the world 'round—Sakharov took the decisive step of putting his thoughts on paper in the milestone essay, "Reflections on Progress, Peaceful Coexistence, and Intellectual Freedom."

The work coincided with a turning point in the development of the dissident movement, the Prague Spring of 1968, the rise and spectacular fall of "socialism with a human face."

"Reflections" defined the direction Sakharov's activism would take from that point on. For the epigraph, Sakharov chose a line from Goethe: "He alone is worthy of life and freedom / Who each day does battle for them anew."

It was not a call to arms; Sakharov did not declare that struggle and heroic exploits are ends in themselves. They are worthwhile, he wrote, "only insofar as they enable other people to lead normal, peaceful lives."

"The meaning of life is life itself," he continued, "that daily routine which demands its own form of unobtrusive heroism."

From this moment on, Sakharov's life moved inexorably toward the recognition of the central importance of openness, justice, and human rights in shaping a normal life.

The essay also introduced Sakharov to the West. As his activism gathered pace, he was often perceived by the outside world as a Russian Don Quixote, a tousled, retiring intellectual who had built a doomsday weapon and was now tilting at the windmills of an all-powerful state.

But his friends saw a different Sakharov—a brilliant, profound, and courageous thinker who, in his purity of vision, posed a fundamental challenge to the state simply by calling *evil* by its name and demanding that the state abide by its own laws.

After he met and married Elena Bonner, who so effectively complemented his stature and intellect with her experience in resistance and activism, the Sakharovs became a beacon of hope for thousands of people caught up in the arbitrary injustice of totalitarianism.

They also became a clearinghouse of information to the outside world. It was enough for Sakharov to appear at the trial of a dissident and to speak to Western reporters to undermine the elaborately concocted accusations. And it was through Sakharov and Bonner that much of the information about the plight of Jews, Tatars, Germans, Russians, believers, and others came to the attention of the world.

It was inevitable that the state would finally act; and, in the end, the great scientist who once had the power to call Khrushchev, Brezhnev, and Andropov on their direct lines was sent into internal exile in an apartment in Gorky, isolated and monitored day and night.

In exile he became an even more powerful force, a symbol of nonviolent opposition in the tradition of Nelson Mandela or Mahatma Gandhi. But it is important to note that his power was never in some ideology or teachings, not in something that disciples would call Sakharovism, like the moral teachings of Tolstoyism or the Holy Russia of Aleksandr Solzhenitsyn. His power was in his example, his moral purity, his openness.

Sakharov didn't even like the word "dissident," probably because the thrust of the human-rights movement was to compel the Soviet Union to live by its own rules, not to challenge the system or change it.

When the human-rights movement first gained momentum, the term Russians used was *pravozashchitniki,* defenders of the law, or *inakomyslyashchie,* which literally means "those who think differently." The West began referring to them as "dissidents" and, in the Russian pronunciation, dissident came into general Russian usage.

What kind of man was he personally? I have found him variously described as naïve, saintly, shy, diffident; to some, he was akin to that Russian character known as *yurodivyi,* the holy fool who speaks truth to power; to others he was the consummate scientist, applying the rigorous discipline of scientific inquiry to politics and human rights.

By all accounts, Sakharov was not easy to work with—people who dealt with him found him stubborn and uncompromising.

He could spend weeks on an essay, as he did with "Reflections," but he could also react on the spur of the moment.

Sakharov was indeed shy and uncomfortable in social settings, but he certainly did not avoid confrontations, making his thoughts clear to the entire Academy of Science when he decided to oppose the nomination of a Lysenko ally, or pushing his way into a courtroom packed with KGB plants where a dissident was about to be tried.

I remember those trials well, though the ones I covered occurred after Sakharov was already in exile in Gorky—no matter how early we arrived, the courtroom was "full," with room only for immediate relatives. We'd stand around outside, waiting for the inevitable conviction.

For those who see him as a meek, retiring, and compassionate genius in the mold of Fyodor Dostoyevsky's Prince Myshkin, I'd like to recall one incredible incident he describes in his *Memoirs*.

Without any advance warning, Sakharov is paid a surprise visit in Gorky by Nikolai Yakovlev, one of the sleazy, corrupted writers used by the KGB to slander its targets. Yakovlev had written an especially foul book attacking Sakharov and making vile anti-Semitic insinuations about his wife, Elena Bonner, yet here he comes and offers to interview Sakharov.

Here's how Sakharov describes what happens next: "I'd realized right away that I was going to end up hitting him."

And sure enough, Sakharov abruptly interrupts the conversation and says, "I'd rather take care of this matter by slapping you.

"I dodged around the table. He flinched and avoided the blow, but I surprised him with an unexpected left-handed slap on his flabby cheek. 'Now get out of here,' I yelled, pushing the door open."

I love to imagine that scene: so much for the passive holy fool.

There's another passage near the end of the *Memoirs* that has long intrigued me. It is about that extraordinary phone call from Mikhail Gorbachev on December 16, 1986. You have to understand that Sakharov has been in exile in Gorky for almost seven years, without a telephone and largely isolated from any contacts, and suddenly a pair of technicians come in at night and hook up a phone and tell him to expect a call in the morning.

"Hello, this is Gorbachev speaking."

"Hello, I'm listening."

Gorbachev then tells Sakharov that his trials are over, that he and Lyusia—the name he and most everyone used for Elena Bonner—can come home to Moscow. So what does Sakharov do? He starts talking to Gorbachev about the recent death of the dissident Anatoly Marchenko in prison, he starts demanding that Gorbachev release all prisoners of conscience.

It really is a remarkable exchange, and a remarkable image of Sakharov, instinctively putting the interests of others ahead of his own at a moment of supreme triumph.

But was it a triumph? The sad truth is that the collapse of the Soviet state, which seemed to vindicate everything the dissidents fought for, did not lead to the democratic state they presumed would follow.

Would he be disappointed? Probably yes, but I don't think that's the sort of category he worked in. His approach was to act on what needed to be changed and reformed, and not to succumb to dismay, disappointment, or despair.

Sakharov would be ninety-three now, and I presume he would be enormously active, writing letters and statements about Ukraine, Georgia, Moldova, and on behalf of Sergei Guriev, Vladimir Yevtushenkov, gay people, or the late Sergei Magnitsky.

He certainly did not pause to celebrate or to gloat when the Soviet state collapsed. He died on December 14, 1989, while working on a speech about the rights of suspects in criminal cases. Those were years of a huge upsurge in violent crime in Russia and, typically, Sakharov was thinking to the end about the rights of individuals.

He told Lyusia he was going to take a nap, but when she went into his room later he had passed away.

* * *

As I said at the outset, I never met the man, to my great regret.

I arrived in the Soviet Union as a correspondent on January 1, 1980, and of course one of my priorities was to meet Sakharov. My background is Russian, and we spoke Russian at home and closely followed developments in the Soviet Union.

My father, a Russian Orthodox theologian, had a weekly broadcast to the Soviet Union over Radio Liberty, and already as a boy I remember the thrill of the intellectual and creative "thaw" introduced by Nikita Khrushchev, and the Russian movies and records that began to reach America in those years, and the enormous excitement of reading Solzhenitsyn's *One Day in the Life of Ivan Denisovich.*

The human-rights movement had unfolded while I was an undergraduate in the 1960s—my campus was on the other side of the continent, and we had no palms—and I followed it with a passion.

The year 1980, when I arrived in Moscow as a correspondant, was a low time in US-Soviet relations—not that there had ever been really good times. A few days before our arrival, the Soviets had invaded Afghanistan. Relations with the West plummeted. And with the Moscow Summer Olympics scheduled for that summer, the KGB was hyperactive.

Sakharov, of course, was already known in the West as a dissident. His "Reflections" had come out in the West in 1968; in 1970 he and other dissidents had founded the Committee on Human Rights, he had married Elena Bonner in 1972, and by the time we arrived the dissident movement was Sakharov's primary occupation, and he was a major thorn in the side of the regime.

When I arrived I thought I was ready for the worst. I was friends with George Krimsky, the AP reporter expelled for his close contacts to Sakharov. I thought I knew how the KGB functioned, that every second person was an informer, that we would be listened to and followed. But knowing all this in theory is not the same as seeing it in reality. Nothing really prepared me for what happened January 22.

That was the day on which the authorities finally moved against Sakharov. We first heard about it from Liza Alexeyeva. She was the fiancée of Bonner's son Alexei Semyonov, who had left the Soviet Union, and she managed to get a call to Western reporters as soon as she heard that Sakharov had been seized.

I rushed to the apartment building on Chkalov Street where Sakharov lived—it was a stretch of the ring road now again called Zemlyanoi Val. There was already an army of uniformed and plainclothes officers keeping everyone at bay. But it was more than that—it was an extraordinary display of power and paranoia, of a superpower going to extreme lengths to silence just one man.

Every telephone, private and public, within a radius of at least a kilometer was cut off, as were the phones of all of Sakharov's close colleagues. Traffic was stopped in both directions. As the facts came out, we learned that a special Aeroflot flight was assigned to fly Sakharov and Bonner to Gorky, with only a dozen KGB agents on board.

Sakharov's description of the flight is another one of those passages that I find revealing of the man. Someone else in his place might have focused on the drama and horror of the event, but Sakharov noted that so long as he and Lyusia were together, "we were actually happy." And he also notes, "Normally there's no meal service on short flights, but on this one we were served a first-class dinner."

The extraordinary measures taken by the state to exile Sakharov, including the constant surveillance, the personal jamming station, the innumerable summons and harassments, were a testament to the moral power that Sakharov had come to wield by then.

It was also a testament to the fragility of the totalitarian state, which knew instinctively that someone who spoke the truth posed an existential threat to the system. There are not many figures in modern history who wielded such power—Nelson Mandela did, and perhaps Aung San Suu Kyi in Burma, but who else?

By evening, Liza Alexeyeva and Bonner's formidable mother, Ruth Bonner, a veteran of barricades and the gulag, were allowed to open the door to reporters, and we learned the details—that Sakharov had been stripped of his state awards and flown off to internal exile in Gorky, a city then off-limits to foreigners.

Let me also note here that being stripped of his three Hero of Socialist Labor awards was no small matter. This was a very prestigious and important award in the Soviet Union, and it carried a broad range of important benefits in pay, housing, and travel.

Only 180 people received it twice; a mere sixteen people had three, like Sakharov. The protocol of the award said that if you got it twice, your bust had to be raised in your hometown; if you got it thrice, they were supposed to build a statue in Moscow. None were built for Sakharov in Soviet times.

* * *

For the first period of Sakharov's exile to Gorky, until May 1984, Elena Bonner was allowed to travel freely to Moscow, and she chalked up more than a hundred sleepless nights on the overnight train. In that period I came to know her quite well.

It's hard to remember all the dates from that time, since unfortunately I did not keep a diary, but I remember that for some inexplicable reason, the car following me changed when Lyusia was in town. It was usually a tan Zhiguli—that's the Soviet version of the old Fiat 124 that was the most sought-after sedan in Russia at the time—which would be there waiting whenever I ventured out of our compound on the garden ring. But when Bonner was in town I'd find a bigger and more official Volga.

Why, I don't know. But it demonstrated the premium the KGB placed on Sakharov and Bonner. Maybe, just maybe, the KGB wanted reporters to see Bonner so the world would be reassured that Sakharov was alive and reasonably well.

Another curious fact is that the guards outside her building did not pull an overnight shift, so that I would come after 2 a.m., often to find an apartment full of friends and foul cigarette smoke. Maybe the idea was to keep the visits as hidden as possible, or to make Sakharov's friends suffer. But the Russian intelligentsia habitually sat around late into the night, so for the Russians it was normal.

My visits were primarily to learn about Sakharov's state. But the apartment on Chkalov Street also remained a clearinghouse for dissident information, as it had been when Sakharov lived there. There was always a dissident from some far-off province who had come to seek help, and they would often hand out fuzzy carbon copies of some declaration.

Some of the visitors were anxious, and talked only in the bath-room with the faucet running, to hide the conversation from the microphones that no doubt were everywhere. Lyusia herself dispensed with any such precautions, as had Sakharov, speaking openly and loudly in full knowledge that the KGB was listening to every word.

That was part of their approach, which differed radically from that of dissidents like Solzhenitsyn, who went to extraordinary measures to keep his conversations secret from the KGB. For the Sakharovs, there was no conspiracy, no secrecy, to their work: their whole point was that what they were doing was fully legal under Soviet law. They were not calling for rebellion, or regime change, or even different laws; only for obedience to the existing law, and that they not only did not want to hide, but they wanted the authorities to hear.

Lyusia was a remarkable woman. Let me quote here from a piece I did about her when she died in June 2011, age eighty-eight: "She was an imposing presence with her thick glasses, and a loud, clear voice that carried the authority of a sergeant-major—she had been an officer on the front. She could be quite forceful with reporters—she would demand that we publish her communiqués verbatim or not at all.

"But at times she was also ready to sit back with a cigarette and a dreamy smile and talk about being a front-line medic in World War II, about her postwar life as a pediatrician and a believing Communist Party member, about her two children, and about her final conversion to open dissent after the Prague Spring of 1968, the date from which the Soviet human-rights movement truly dates."

I would also turn to Bonner for help. One of my strongest recollections is not connected to Sakharov, but to a dissident named Vladimir Borisov who had been expelled to the West for his effort to create a free trade union. In July 1980, I got a call from his wife, Irina Kaplun, asking to see me.

She was on her way to catch a train to Tallinn, Estonia, and as we walked to the train station, a man popped up from behind a car and photographed us. She passed on some information and went on her way. On the next day, I learned that she had been killed in a car crash on arrival to Estonia. From abroad, her husband accused the KGB of murder.

Bonner was in Moscow, and she went directly to Tallinn. She called on her return to tell me that there was no question that it was a real road accident. Certainly the dissident cause would have been advanced by letting suspicions fester and letting the Kremlin squirm, but Bonner and Sakharov always saw their strength in speaking truth, not in propaganda.

That was the way the Sakharovs were. Though their own lives in Gorky were intolerable, marked by excruciating hunger strikes, isolation, and harassment, they continued to the best of their ability to help others, whether dissidents or their kin.

I must note here that while I have very strong and fond memories of Elena Bonner, I am not sure what impression I left on her. In November 1985, I flew to Italy with her when she was finally allowed to leave the country for treatment of glaucoma and heart problems, and we talked the whole way over about their lives in Gorky, the success of their hunger strikes in getting the authorities to let Liza Alexeyeva, now Bonner's daughter-in-law, emigrate, and about everything else that was happening.

In her memoirs, however, Elena Bonner wrote that she had no memory of the flight over. Frankly, since all I did was to prompt her memories, there is no reason she should remember, and I remain grateful for all the time I spent with her.

I only wish I could have spent as much with Sakharov. But by the time he was released, I was stationed in Germany, and by the time I returned to Russia for another stint, he had died.

* * *

I'd like to say a few words about Sakharov's legacy. Sakharov's own path from a willing servant of the state to a dissident willing to starve himself to death for a young woman's right to emigrate was hardly rapid or linear, as I've already noted. It took his thinking decades to evolve from the belief in the Soviet state as the prototype for the future world, to a sense that all governments are bad, and finally to the realization that the messianic pretensions of the Soviet state created a unique system of totalitarian repression.

At the outset of his career at Arzamas, the super-secret "Installation" in which he worked on the Bomb, a lot of the lesser work was done by *zeks,* gulag inmates who were marched to and from their jobs, fed pathetic rations, and housed in crowded barracks. Sakharov was aware of them and their plight, yet it took many more years before this grotesque violation of human rights became one of his causes.

I would argue that this was not hypocrisy—not a deliberate blindness to the suffering of others. I think we in the West too often underestimate the fundamental patriotism that motivated Russians to fight so valiantly against Nazi Germany, and we too often underestimate the idealism that existed among Soviet citizens, Communists and non-Communists.

Elena Bonner was proud of her party card, as were many of the dissidents I met. And Sakharov, though he declined to join the party, was an uncritical believer in the merits of socialism over capitalism until his eyes opened to the violations of human rights.

For him, as for virtually all Soviet citizens, World War II—the Great Patriotic War—was an elemental struggle for survival. It remains to this day one of the most powerful collective memories among Russians; it is not accidental that Putin refers to Ukrainian nationalists as fascists or invokes other images of the Great War.

Sakharov himself had been hustled to the rear to work on munitions, and fully shared in the sense of urgency and sacrifice of a nation fighting for survival.

In that world, Stalin was first and foremost a war leader, who not only had to pull Russia through a mortal threat but had to build up its power after the war so that it could not be attacked again.

I spoke with many older Russians when I lived there, and especially when I was writing a book about the village of my ancestors. The sense of collective sacrifice and heroic struggle was a recurring theme.

Like those people, Sakharov knew of the crimes committed under Stalin, and he was aware of the *zeks* working alongside him, but all that was subordinate to the national sense that the times required sacrifice and suffering.

That applied also to the awesome weapon Sakharov was developing. This is what he wrote:

"I understood, of course, the terrifying, inhuman nature of the weapons we were building. But the recent war had also been an exercise in barbarity, and although I hadn't fought in that conflict, I regarded myself as a soldier in this new scientific war."

The passage ends, as do so many of his other efforts to explain the evolution of his political thinking, with: "The truth is never simple."

* * *

I am not trying to justify or to defend Sakharov. God knows he does not need my defense or justification. But in the years I spent in the Soviet Union and in Russia, I tried to understand how people survived through the combined hell of Stalinism and the war, how people maintained their integrity, how they survived.

The dissidents were only a small part of that complex truth, but they were an enormously demanding group, who saw Western journalists as their allies in a struggle with a totalitarian system. They certainly deserved support. And trying to get their stories out to the West entailed huge risk. After Yuri Andropov, a long-time head of the KGB, became the Soviet leader in November 1982, the repression became even heavier as the KGB began systematically rounding up members of the human-rights movement.

To this day I suffer over the decisions I had to make on what to report and what not to report. I confess Lyusia often chided me harshly for not dedicating myself exclusively to the cause of human rights.

She believed that it was our duty, our obligation—as free men and women residing in the Soviet Union—to dedicate ourselves to the cause of human rights. The notion of journalists as objective, neutral witnesses was alien to the dissidents, as it was to the authorities who saw us as tools of Western propaganda.

And to be honest, the entire notion of neutrality or objectivity was hard to define in a society where reporting the reality was in itself a political act, and where all sides saw us as soldiers in the Cold War.

I remember a diplomat at the American Embassy, presumably from the CIA, demanding that I give him the names of some Russian sources of mine. When I refused, he angrily asked, "What side are you on, Schmemann?"

Throughout my years there, my guidance was something that Lydia Chukovskaya, the daughter of Russia's favorite children's author, Kornei Chukovsky, told me when I first visited her in the large dacha in Peredelkino which she maintained as a museum to her father.

Lydia was an author and active dissident herself, but what she said was this: "Yes, do not neglect the dissidents. But never forget that there are 268 million other people who wake up every morning in this country who are not dissidents."

That struck me forcibly because I could not be sure what I would have been had my grandparents not left after the revolution. I suspect I would've been among the 268 million, trying to survive with as much integrity as I could but falling short of the martyrdom that dissidence amounted to.

These are the people who interested me, the people who tried to maintain a modicum of self-respect and integrity in a system that demanded total fealty.

And surviving in that system was not necessarily moral failure. Though the active, known dissidents numbered a minuscule percentage of the population, the large majority of people I met resisted the system to the degree they could, listening to the foreign short-wave radio broadcasts, reading and copying the *samizdat* literature, secretly baptizing their

Andrei Sakharov and Sidney Drell, Stanford University, 1989. Photo by Harvey Lynch.

children, studying Hebrew, writing "for the drawer," as the expression went.

One of the many great books published when glasnost made it possible was *Notes of a Survivor* by Sergei Golitsyn. He was a member of a princely family that ended up stranded in the Soviet Union and suffered for it. Such aristocrats who survived were forever reminded that they were *byvshye lyudi*, the former people.

Golitsyn describes being a small boy in the 1920s when one after another of his uncles and aunts were taken away for questioning, some never to return. He recalls assuming that his turn would eventually come and wondering how he would behave. He resolved that whatever else happened, he would never renounce his belief in God.

That was his red line, and I know many other people had a red line in their conscience, a point beyond which they would refuse to answer or cooperate. By the time I got to the Soviet Union in the 1980s, the KGB had become quite sophisticated about finding that red line and pushing people right up to it, but not over it. Many people who were questioned became so determined not to divulge what they had vowed to defend that they failed to realize how much the KGB was getting out of them. The KGB was damned good at interrogations.

By the same token, many honest people who never wanted to become a dissident became one because they were pushed to the limits. People like Lev Kopelev, who had sat in the camps, was an earnest Communist who only wanted to study German culture afterward. But as one after another of his friends was arrested or exiled, he finally signed a protest and was himself sent into exile.

For some people who struggled to function within the system, the moral absolutism of the dissidents was an irritant, a constant moral judgment on their own acceptance of the phony elections, party meetings, and innumerable other acts of fealty and obedience demanded by the state.

One of Sakharov's superiors, Efim Slavsky, summed up this attitude when he assailed Sakharov for turning against the system he had served: "Without a strong hand"—that was Stalin, of course—"we could never have rebuilt our economy after the war or broken the American atomic monopoly—you yourself helped do that. You have no moral right to judge our generation—Stalin's generation—for its mistakes, for its brutality, you're now enjoying the fruits of our labor and our sacrifice."

Slavsky might have noticed, too, that many of the best-known dissidents were scientists who could have lived quite comfortably had they not challenged the system. Yuri Orlov, Sergei Kovalev, and Valery Chalidze, for example, were prominent or promising physicists.

That is not a coincidence, for reasons I know will be discussed here in coming days: science is by its very nature international, questioning, rational, and therefore inherently resistant to ideology and myths. Lysenko and his pseudoscientific ideas were of course a glaring example of ideology co-opting science, but Lysenko was the exception that proves the rule.

For these scientists, many of whom worked on programs to assure the security of the Soviet state, the evolution of their thinking was a continuation of their scientific inquiry, complete with doubts and questions.

"I am not a professional politician," Sakharov wrote. "Perhaps that is why I am always burdened by doubt about the usefulness and consequences of my actions. I incline to the belief that a combination of moral criteria and unrestricted inquiry provides the only possible compass."

A common criticism, made by Solzhenitsyn and some other dissidents, was that Sakharov spread himself too thin, that he took on campaigns that did not advance the cause, whether it was the human-rights movement, or science, or the cause of people.

The criticism became especially sharp when Sakharov and Bonner began a hunger strike to win an exit visa for Liza Alexeyeva, Bonner's daughter-in-law. They won, but many dissidents assailed Sakharov for risking his life over a trivial family affair.

An even stronger, and far more pernicious, criticism was that Sakharov was somehow deflected from his true cause by Elena Bonner. These insinuations were spread by the KGB, with distinct anti-Semitic overtones, based on the fact that Bonner was half-Jewish—her Armenian half was never invoked. It also came from the pen of Solzhenitsyn, leading to a conflict between the two giants of dissent.

Bonner certainly was tough and uncompromising, and I don't doubt she told Andrei exactly what she thought. She was born to fiery Communists who were repressed in the purges, she was steeled by war, and she welcomed the fight. She enjoyed telling me the story of how she knocked down a policeman who tried to push her away at the trial of Yuri Orlov. It was a skill, she said, that she developed fending off overly friendly soldiers at the front, and it landed her in jail for fifteen days.

But to portray Sakharov as someone who could be manipulated by her simply overlooks his history before he met Bonner, and his personality. This is a man who had confronted Politburo members face-to-face. And as his thinking evolved—through opposition to Lysenko, through the realization of the deathly danger of nuclear tests, through support of people he believed were being mistreated by the authorities—he never hesitated to speak out and act, whatever the potential danger to his own career.

Of course, he was not a saint; he himself acknowledged many dubious decisions; but there was an astounding clarity to his thought and to his morals. He was simply not the kind of man who could be manipulated.

His relationship with Lyusia was something quite different. It was on one level a true love affair. To read their accounts of each other, or to hear Lyusia talking about Andrei, as I often did, there was no question of a deep love.

I remember Lyusia telling me she had to get back to Gorky because Andrei was fixated on a physics problem, and at such times, she said, he simply forgot to eat. And when she talked about him, her face would break into a gentle smile.

Bonner and Sakharov were on two very different and separate tracks that merged in the human-rights movement. She was a hereditary rebel, daughter of ardent Communists and veterans of the gulag, a war veteran and fearless warrior. He was the elite scientist moving steadily toward an awareness of the inherent injustice of the system.

Their paths converged, symbolically, at a dissident trial in 1970, and merged a year later, so that what Sakharov did thereafter, and what Bonner did, was one action.

Sakharov did not think in terms of abstract and grand causes, or of his own role as a symbol or leader. Liza may have been the immediate reason for the hunger strike, he wrote in his *Memoirs*, "but in a broader sense, it was the consequence of all that had happened to us, including exile in Gorky, and a continuation of my struggle for human rights and the freedom to choose one's country of residence—not in the abstract, but in a situation in which Lyusia and I had from the beginning felt a direct responsibility."

This is also at the core of the contrast between Sakharov and Solzhenitsyn. They came to it from radically different directions.

For Solzhenitsyn, everything he did and everything he expected of other people was subordinate to his mission, which was based on an idealized Russian character and religion. I saw that first-hand when Solzhenitsyn first arrived in the United States, because in the beginning he was very close to my father, an Orthodox theologian. But it soon became clear that Solzhenitsyn had little interest in my father's work in America, which involved the Orthodox Church in America. What concerned him was Russia, holy and great.

In an article Sakharov wrote in response to Solzhenitsyn's "Letter to Soviet Leaders," he warned that politicians who follow in the footsteps of ideologues tend to be more dogmatic and ruthless than their mentors. There's something prophetic in that warning, given how Vladimir Putin, who was blessed by Solzhenitsyn, has built his politics around the notion of Russian greatness and destiny.

It was in the clash with Solzhenitsyn that Andrei Sakharov provided what I think is the best description of himself and his legacy. "I'm no politician, no prophet, and certainly no angel," he wrote. "What I've done and what I am are not the result of any miracle but the natural consequences of what life has made me. . . . It may be a peculiarity of my character, but I've never lived in luxury, and I'm not even sure what it is. . . . As I never tire of repeating, life is a complicated thing.

"Most important," he concluded, "I have tried to be true to myself and my destiny."

That is Sakharov's real legacy: his honesty, his greatness, his genius, his integrity, his compassion for individuals.

He did not, alas, leave behind a Russia democratic and free. That may take generations.

Hopefully, Andrei Dmitrievich will continue to serve as a beacon and a model for those generations.

The Scientist as Prophet: Sakharov's World and Ours

J. Bryan Hehir

There is an ancient principle of spiritual wisdom in the Christian tradition that "confession is good for the soul." I am going to follow that advice by confessing how much I do not know about Andrei Sakharov. I never met him and never heard him lecture. I know no Russian and I'm not much better in physics, so I have not attempted to understand his world-famous accomplishments. From a great distance—and from listening to Sid Drell—I admired his role in the nuclear age. It is because of Sid's invitation that I agreed to be part of a project with respected colleagues who knew Andrei Sakharov in ways I never did.

Having agreed, I considered what I might usefully contribute. My chapter title is an attempt at an answer. Sakharov was by talent and *vocation* a Nobel Prize scientist. He was by *avocation* an engaged moral critic of the very age he helped to produce—the nuclear age. Not being able to illuminate his proper vocation, I have set out to describe the meaning of his avocation: the scientist as prophet.

In the nuclear age scientists have been the ultimate insiders. Whether it was in Washington or Moscow, scientists possessed the knowledge which was the golden coin of the realm in the nuclear age. They were sought after, listened to, celebrated, and drawn

21

into the core secrets of both superpowers. Prophets are hardly ever insiders; what they have to offer is often not good news for those who hold power. So, my goal is to test the tension between Sakharov's vocation and his avocation. He was not alone in experiencing this tension: political leaders and scientists shared the experience. In the United States Sakharov had counterparts, some of whom described their experiences in powerful testimonies. Victor "Viki" Weisskopf, professor of physics at MIT, reflected on his involvement in the Manhattan Project fifty years later:

> Thinking back to those eventful years at Los Alamos, from 1943–1945, evokes two opposite feelings. On one side it was a heroic period of our lives, full of the most exciting problems and achievements. We worked within an international community of the best and most productive scientists in the world, facing a stupendous task fraught with many unknown ramifications. . . . On the other side, we must be deeply aware of the result of our work. . . . The bomb did end the cruel and destructive war with Japan, but since then it has developed into the greatest danger that humankind has ever faced, and it threatens more and more to destroy everything on earth that we consider worth living for.[1]

Over time, moving away from the events of Hiroshima and Nagasaki, the nuclear age—in East and West—came to be seen in this light. Human ingenuity had unlocked a power which human politics seemed unable to fully master. The memory of what had happened continued to haunt the historical experience of the most powerful nations in the world. Sakharov was a central participant in this drama.

The purpose here is, first, to describe the role of prophecy in any setting; second, to sketch the context in which Sakharov functioned; and third, to contrast our age with his.

The Vocation of the Prophet

The intent here is not to celebrate prophets uncritically; some of them have been deeply misguided. Even when accurate, their advice cannot and should not always be followed. I invoke three varied descriptions of a prophetic posture in human affairs.

First, the home of our common understanding of prophecy resides in the Hebrew Bible where we encounter the great prophetic voices: Isaiah, Jeremiah, Amos, and Hosea.[2] In the community of Israel the prophets emerged six to eight centuries before the Common Era. Often they were in conflict and tension with the kings and priests in Israel; the former ruled the nation, the latter were responsible for the community's worship. The prophet's role was distinct from both. Technically, the word prophet meant one who spoke for God. They were not adept at forecasting the future; they were instead those who saw deeply into the meaning of the present. They were the moral conscience of the community, those who recalled it to its roots when kings and priests had lost their way. The prophets spoke to protect "the orphans and the widows and the resident aliens" when those in power failed in their duties. The prophets also criticized worship devoid of moral rectitude in daily life. Finally, like Isaiah, they sought to keep alive the vision of peace for a people who (even then) lived in conflicted territory.

Two characteristics of prophetic discourse often rendered them "outsiders": first, their standard message was cast as a moral absolute; second, they aimed at conversion (deep and immediate) rather than pedagogical persuasion.

Because the prophets believed they had clear insight into the mind and will of God for Israel, their posture vis-à-vis the king or the priest or the community as a whole was "thus saith the Lord." Because they were mandated to bring about the will of God, the prophets sought nothing short of conversion of mind and heart. Neither patience nor negotiation with secular or priestly power was usual for them.

Sakharov's *style* does not sound prophetic; his friends and colleagues convey a sense of courage, intelligence, and humility. But his positions on nuclear testing, arms control, and coexistence, all advocated at the height of the Cold War, must have set him apart from the dominant political discourse in the upper regions of Soviet policymaking. Even without the prophetic *style* one can become an "outsider" because of the *substance* of a moral or political position. Others in this volume can describe more clearly the content of his prophetic positions.

The Hebrew scriptures originated in a very different culture and mindset from the twentieth century. But the role of the prophet survived in adapted form in the modern era. A second description of the voice of an "outsider" is reflected in one of the founders of modern social science, Max Weber, the prolific German sociologist. Weber to some degree was an insider *and* outsider in German political life. In one of his most famous essays, "Politics as a Vocation," Weber analyzes the intersection of ethics and political choice. He sets the context by warning that politics is not a vocation to choose if one wishes to save one's soul. Then he proceeds to distinguish two conceptions of ethics in politics: the "ethic of ultimate ends" and the "ethic of responsibility."[3] In the language of modern philosophical ethics, the positions might be described as deontological (Kantian) and consequentialist (Bentham, et al.). Here again, in Weber's concepts, the distinction is between a position that admits of no compromise on certain issues (like the pacifist on war) versus a position which acknowledges a world in which *some* balancing of consequences (cost/benefit in style) is necessary for morally responsible action. The fact that Weber, in his essay, ultimately acknowledges that *some* mix of the two positions is needed for any ethic of public affairs does not alter the difference in style and content between them. The "ethic of responsibility" is implicitly or explicitly affirmed in most policy debates. To hold an "ethic of ultimate ends" is to assume the outsider's perspective even if one is in the inner circle of policy debate.

It would take more research on the specifics of Sakharov's role in policymaking to identify carefully where he stood in Weber's terms. Given what happened to him in the Soviet system, his views may have functionally been the prophet's, sounding absolutistic and nonnegotiable. One could note here that Robert Oppenheimer stands as a similar case in the United States. His plea to President Harry S. Truman not to proceed with the hydrogen bomb instantly made him an outsider whom Truman no longer wanted to hear from in spite of his unique role in the Manhattan Project.

The point here is a modest one, simply to describe that within the policy process individuals who have standing because of their office, knowledge, and expertise or their reputation in a field can create powerful tensions and conflicts by staking out a moral position which lies far ahead or outside of what is to be taken as "realistic" or "established" policy. Testimony to this phenomenon is the perspective of a scholar and participant at the highest levels of US decision making, Dr. Henry Kissinger. Reflecting on his initial impressions about moving from the academy to the White House, Kissinger wrote that his first task was "to learn the difference between a conclusion and a policy." He then went on to comment on the insider/outsider relationship regarding morality:

> But I believed equally that no nation could form or even define its choices without a moral compass that set a course through the ambiguities of reality and thus made sacrifices meaningful. The willingness to walk this fine line marks the difference between the academic's—or any outsider's—perception of morality and that of the statesman. The outsider thinks in terms of absolutes, for him right and wrong are defined in their conception. The political leader does not have this luxury. He can rarely reach his goal except in stages, any partial step is inherently morally imperfect and yet morality cannot be approximated without it. The philosopher's test is the reasoning behind his maxims, the statesman's test is not only the exaltation of his goals but the catastrophe he averts.[4]

Kissinger's comments are useful in the sense that they represent the classical insider's perspective. To some degree, however, he states the insider's case in extreme and cryptic fashion. Rather than engage the substantive position of the critic, he reduces the clash to purely functional terms. This marginalizes the possibility that in some cases the ethic of absolute ends provides the best "moral compass" for the policymaker. Critiques about decisions

Kissinger made—not usually about nuclear issues, but about human rights, covert action, and Vietnam—are reminders that a purely functional resolution of Weber's distinction fails to take the outsider's perspective seriously.

From the fate he suffered at times, Sakharov must have sounded like the prophetic outsider to Soviet statesmen.

Sakharov's Normative Issues

Andrei Sakharov brought together two great issues in his role of moral critic: nuclear weapons and human rights. The two issues shared one characteristic and yet differed in content. Their similarity resided in the fact that both issues arose initially in the 1940s, products of World War II and responses to it. War had been a perennial feature of human history but *nuclear war* redefined much of the strategic and moral landscape. Human rights, a perennial *moral* question, took on new political-legal meaning with the founding of the United Nations. Sakharov's voice became globally significant on both issues. Commonality of origin then diverged about content. The nuclear question was cosmic in scope and densely technological in composition; it rested primarily in the control of the superpowers. Human rights, while universal in scope, were primarily a philosophical-legal question affecting every person's welfare. Sakharov's testimony encompassed both the cosmic and personal issues. In this way he was a unique moral witness in the 1970s and 1980s. Bishop Swing is addressing the human rights issue; here I will focus on the nature of the nuclear question to which Sakharov was tied personally as a creator and a critic.

The political and strategic complexity of the nuclear age was evident from its beginning. The moral complexity, less fulsomely addressed in the beginning, was equally dense and difficult to resolve. War has never been a purely political-strategic question; from Thucydides to Leo Tolstoy to Winston Churchill, war's moral conduct has always been part of the human equation. The dominant moral lens, evident in Sakharov's time and in ours, has been the "just-war ethic."[5] Taken as a whole, the ethic reflects

Weber's recognition that an adequate political ethic must combine absolute principles *and* a counting of consequences. In a world where both human nature and human history testified to the need for some coercive restraint of injustice, the just-war ethic's assessment of consequences led to its basic assertion that *some* use of force could be moral. Embedded in that logic, however, lay the absolute principle that directly intended targeting and killing of civilians was never permissible. The ethic confronted the diverse forms of warfare from the Roman Empire to the world wars of the last century. But Hiroshima and Nagasaki opened a new chapter in human history.

Science, politics, and strategy had produced qualitative change in human destructive capability. Sakharov, like Weisskopf and Oppenheimer, stood at the intersection of science and strategy. The record indicates that in the immediate aftermath of the war no one had clear, compelling answers to what to do about what had been produced and exploded in 1945. Michael Mandelbaum, in *The Nuclear Question*,[6] charts the debates and decisions within the American policy community of scientists, strategists, and political leaders.

Initially, two polar positions existed: to treat nuclear weapons as ordinary and usable or to advocate for disarmament of nuclear weapons (or locate them in the control of international authority). Neither position could bear the weight of the nuclear age. As Thomas Schelling said in his Nobel Prize Lecture, early on elite opinion and public opinion recognized that nuclear weapons were unique. But they also were not to be dispelled by diplomacy: in the language of the policy debate, the world would have to learn to live *with* nuclear weapons, before it found a way to live *without* them.[7] As Mandelbaum and others have documented, the nuclear debate by the 1960s had reached a consensus on the dual policies of deterrence and arms control. Neither of the original polar positions had been vindicated.

The policy of deterrence and arms control posed its own challenges for the moral doctrine on war. It clearly was an advance over the position that nuclear weapons were normal and simply available to states. Deterrence sought to forestall use without simply conceding to one's adversary. Arms control sought to contain and control the competition of nuclear states. But embedded in the doctrine of deterrence was a clear willingness to use nuclear weapons in a "second strike" if necessary. This determination raised two questions. First, what targeting doctrine would direct such a response? Could it pass the *jus in bello* principles? Second, what of the intention of the policy? The issue here, which engaged only some moralists, was whether a firm intent to use nuclear weapons against civilian centers was already a severe moral problem even if use never occurred.[8]

The positions moralists took spread across a spectrum. Some who held to just-war teaching in the prenuclear age used the doctrine now to conclude that nuclear weapon and deterrence policy could never pass the twin principles of *jus in bello* (i.e., noncombatant immunity and proportionality). They became "nuclear pacifists," opposing both *use* and *deterrence*. Consequentialist moralists (Weber's ethic of responsibility) found in deterrence an acceptable moral position; the intentionality issue did not weigh substantially in consequentialist logic, and the stability which deterrence seemed to provide outweighed the risks it posed. A third position was a modified absolutist ethic: it held that nuclear weapons could never be targeted on cities but a counterforce deterrent, strictly defined, would be both acceptable (at least tolerable) and would provide guidance for targeting doctrine.

The basic moral positions, like the strategic discourse they resembled, yielded a pluralism of policy conclusions. Sakharov came to the nuclear debate as a scientist, but he obviously saw in the nuclear threat a challenge that was not the property of moralists alone.

My sense is that his moral critique was derived not from formal philosophical or theological positions, but from the depth of his understanding of what nuclear weapons were capable of doing. The moral position, I suspect, was rooted in scientific insight. As a scientist he was "inside" the nuclear debate in a way few people were. But his inside perspective placed him at least partially outside the parameters of existing policy. For his courage in testing both science and strategy by a humane morality, he paid the prophet's price.

Sakharov's World and Ours

As we honor Sakharov's scholarship, values, and personal witness at this conference, it is also necessary to assess how his world differed from ours today in both its factual and moral challenges. The differences do not prohibit learning from Sakharov's intellect and courage, and they may help us decide how his witness can guide choices at a different time.

Sakharov's time—the intellectual and political setting for his work—was decidedly the Cold War. The Cold War world was politically bipolar and strategically nuclear, an international system that was highly structured, with clear lines drawn and alliances shaped (East and West) to support the interests of the superpowers. It was the world of "the two, the few, and the many": the two super-states, the few allied with them, and the sweeping geography and cultures of the many in the Southern Hemisphere. Looked at from our time, the world conveys a dangerous but well-defined clarity and stability. Such a description fails to capture the complexity which lay beneath both the clarity and the stability, but it does identify some basic truths of world politics from 1949 to 1989.

The world of today, our time, provides sharp contrasts. The cosmic threat of a massive nuclear exchange has declined, but the legacy of nuclear weapons remains in more differentiated force. The world is less state-centric, with differing views of whether this is an asset or a new danger for world order. The world of our time, reviewed in light of the last twenty years, can produce three distinct kinds of conflicts: the possibility of classic interstate war remains, but with reduced likelihood; the combined issues of internal conflict and outside intervention have multiplied; and the advent of transnational terrorism, enhanced by the interdependence of states, has recast much of strategic discourse. The problems of our time have regional sources but potentially global implications; to some degree they seem smaller but less open to a single definition or a broader comprehensive strategy ("wars on terror" are not adequate).

Our time can certainly use more Sakharov types, combining technical expertise with moral vision and courage, but it is not clear where such persons would focus their attention. The problems are diverse in nature, not necessarily related in their resolution; and they admit of differing timelines, some immediate and others reaching well out into this still-young century.

Colleagues at this conference who knew Sakharov as I never did will be able to sort out the resources he left us to address questions he never faced. In this final section I can only offer a perspective on some of the ways our world differs from his.

1. Changes in the structure of power and principles of order. I have argued in other writings that a major consequence of the transition to a post-Cold War world has been the intersection of changes in the hierarchy of states and changes in basic concepts of world order. The collapse of bipolarity yielded a debate which continues today: what has taken its place? The answers have ranged from unipolarity (Charles Krauthammer) to nonpolarity (Richard Haass) to a more complex picture of a three-dimensional universe combining military unipolarity, political multipolarity, and pluralism among states and other global actors (Joseph S. Nye).[9] Changes in the structure of power historically have created complex and, at times, dangerous moments in world politics. Twenty years after the collapse of the Cold War, a rising China, a still-evolving Russia, and a less-than-clear United States are major reasons—but not the only ones—why a consensus about today's structure of power is elusive.

Understanding changes in the principles of order takes us back to the beginning of the modern state system. The seventeenth-century Westphalian order produced three basic ideas: the sovereignty of states, the principle of nonintervention, and the secularization of world politics. In the last forty years, multiple factors have eroded the secure status each of these ideas has held in world politics. State sovereignty has been eroded, ceding ground to economic interdependence, human rights claims, and the role of international institutions. Erosion does not at all mean elimination—but it has changed the effective capacity of states. In the 1990s, the multiple internal conflicts of states (rooted in politics, ethnicity, and religion) raised anew questions about the legitimacy of *humanitarian* military intervention by states, regional organizations, or the United Nations. The outcome of these debates and interventionary decisions has not produced a new consensus internationally, but it has produced the idea of "responsibility to protect,"[10] a significant revision of the Westphalian model which still remains short of customary international law. The third element of Westphalia, more implicit than expressed, was the effort to secularize would politics. In many ways it has succeeded, but not entirely—as I will indicate below. Sakharov lived and worked within an international order where the three concepts of Westphalia were secure; all three are still essential elements of world politics, but each is challenged today.

2. State versus nonstate actions. Flowing directly from the changed status of the Westphalian order of politics is the way in which state sovereignty is now challenged. The challenge arises from the diffusion of state power on the one hand and the rise— in number and diversity—of nonstate actors on the other. States remain the central actors of world politics; but the distinction drawn today between *formal* sovereignty and a more limited *operational* sovereignty highlights the changing status of states. They now have competitors of various kinds, from human rights organizations to the Islamic State. International institutions are created by states, but the states also set boundaries for the institutions' choices. Transnational institutions operate with increasing resources and skill across sovereign boundaries, usually with state consent but sometimes in opposition to state objectives. Nongovernmental actors are rooted within states but collaborate with other organizations beyond the scope of their home states. A radically new chapter in this narrative is the post-9/11 world of Al Qaeda and the Islamic State, transnational nonstate actors which act like states in the military arena. Until 9/11, most attention to nonstate organizations had been focused on socioeconomic and human rights issues, but new issues of global governance and state security have opened since 9/11.

3. Religious actors. Distinct from, but related to, the role of nonstate actors is the return of religious ideas and organizations to international relations. The Westphalian order of world politics was shaped in light of the vivid memory of religious warfare in the sixteenth and seventeenth centuries. Separating religion from interstate politics was a high priority and became a standard assumption of foreign policy in the West. Over the last four decades, a range of different cases has led to what is now being described in diverse quarters as "the resurgence of religion" in world affairs.[11] Situations as distinct as Poland and the Philippines, South Africa and Central America, and the Middle East are permeated by religious themes. The emphasis since 9/11 has focused on Islam and its impact, but it would be a mistake to see this as an isolated case. How religion can and will influence politics—positively or negatively—is a subject that divides analysts. But few believe it now can simply be ignored.

4. Three interlocking macro-problems. The Cold War had a defined, intense, dangerous, and—to some degree—tightly restricted agenda of issues. Political-military issues and the larger ideological contest of East and West absorbed much of the analysis of that era. Today, the agenda of world politics has raised other issues to the level of attention once reserved for diplomats and scholars. Three distinct but interlocking topics illustrate the contemporary agenda. They are: (1) nuclear proliferation and its consequences; (2) globalization and its consequences; (3) environmental threats and their consequences. Sakharov was deeply involved in the first; I'm not aware the other two issues engaged him in any depth. Today, the reduction of each and the way these questions interact represent challenges which define much of "our time."

In light of the theme of this conference, "the conscience of humanity," it is in order to observe that the selective list just noted to distinguish "our time" involves issues which are as deeply moral as they are factually complex. To assess the legitimacy and the limits of sovereignty, to test the proposal to override the nonintervention rule, involves both political wisdom and moral discernment. The three "macro" problems cannot be contained within purely empirical analysis; the consequences of each directly engage the welfare of humanity. Sakharov's work and witness had global reach and consequences. His legacy invites others to imitate his convictions and commitments.

Notes

1. Victor F. Weisskopf, "Looking Back on Los Alamos," in *Assessing the Nuclear Age*, ed. Len Ackland and Steven McGuire (Chicago: Educational Foundation for Nuclear Science, 1986), 23.

2. Bruce Vawter, "Introduction to Prophetic Literature," in *The New Jerome Biblical Commentary*, ed. Raymond Brown, Joseph A. Fitzmyer, and Roland E. Murphy (Englewood Cliffs, NJ: Prentice Hall, 1990), 186–200.

3. Max Weber, "Politics as a Vocation," in *From Max Weber: Essays in Sociology*, ed. H. H. Gerth and C. W. Mills (New York: Oxford University Press, 1958), 46ff.

4. Henry A Kissinger, *The White House Years* (New York: Little Brown, 1979), 55.

5. For examples of the ethic, see Paul Ramsey, *The Just War: Force and Political Responsibility* (New York: Charles Scribner's Sons, 1968); and Michael Walzer, *Just and Unjust Wars: A Moral Argument with Historical Illustrations* (New York: Basic Books, 1977).

6. Michael Mandelbaum, *The Nuclear Question: The United States and Nuclear Weapons, 1946–1976* (Cambridge: Cambridge University Press, 1979).

7. Thomas C. Schelling, "An Astonishing Sixty Years: The Legacy of Hiroshima," *American Economic Review* 96, no. 4 (September 2006): 929–37; and the Harvard Nuclear Study Group (Albert Carnesale, Paul Doty, Stanley Hoffmann, Samuel P. Huntington, Joseph S. Nye Jr., Scott D. Sagan, and Derek Bok), *Living with Nuclear Weapons* (Cambridge, MA: Harvard University Press, 1983).

8. For the preeminent statement of this position, see John Finnis, Joseph Boyle, and Germain Grisez, *Nuclear Deterrence, Morality and Realism* (Oxford: Oxford University Press, 1987).

9. Charles Krauthammer, "The Unipolar Moment," *Foreign Affairs (America and the World)* 70 (1990–91): 23–33; Richard Haass, "The Age of Nonpolarity," *Foreign Affairs* 87 (May–June 2008): 44–56; and Joseph S. Nye, "International Conflicts in the Post-Cold War World," in *Managing Conflict in the Post-Cold War World: The Role of Intervention* (Washington, DC: Aspen Institute, 1996), 63–76.

10. Gareth Evans, *The Responsibility to Protect: Ending Mass Atrocity Crimes Once and for All* (Washington, DC: Brookings Institution Press, 2008), 31–54.

11. See Scott M. Thomas, *The Global Resurgence of Religion and the Transformation of International Relations* (New York: Palgrave Macmillan, 2005); and Monica Duffy Toft, Daniel Philpott, and Timothy Samuel Shah, *God's Century: Resurgent Religion and Global Politics* (New York: W. W. Norton, 2001).

The Soul and Sakharov

William Swing

Without fear of being contradicted, I can say that I am the least qualified person attending this conference to speak about this great man, Andrei Sakharov. Some others at this event knew him, worked with him, or had extensive knowledge of him during his lifetime. I, on the other hand, was in high school—engrossed in sports and agonizing about whom to dance with at the sock hop at Huntington High School in West Virginia—while Andrei Sakharov was laboring on the creation of a hydrogen bomb. Later, at Kenyon College, where each student had to pass one science course, I flunked physics 101 for three straight years. Finally, my professor took me aside a week before graduation to predict that I might just do something worthwhile with my life but it would certainly not be in the field of physics. So he gave me D minus-minus to move me along. Now I blush to begin a paper on this eminent physicist.

If "fresh eyes" are a gift in our memorial focus, then perhaps, in that, I qualify. But more to the point, as a priest and, later, as a bishop, I bring a lifetime spent wrestling with moral and spiritual issues in the realm of life and death, interpreting sacred writings and classic myths, and taking public stands on matters affecting society. Among those issues, nuclear weapons abolition and expansion of human rights have never been far from my sight in the past fifty years. Parts of Andrei Sakharov's story resonate with parts of my story. Therefore, armed with a faith perspective and an abiding sympathy for the guiding moral issues that fueled his passion, I began a research into the writings by and about Andrei Sakharov. What jumped out at me were three distinct perspectives of his life, each one anchored in a different posture toward religious faith: A believing time. An atheistic time. And an agnostic, humanistic time.

Sakharov: The Fashioning of His Soul

As one might expect, I started out looking for a thread of religion in his story. My first exploration had to do with standard Russian Orthodox observances. For instance, was Sakharov baptized? Coming from a long line of Orthodox parish priests, he most likely was baptized. But no one mentioned this, including Sakharov himself. His mother, Katya Sofiano, and his father, Dmitri Sakharov, were married on July 1, 1918, at the Assumption on the Graves Church in Moscow. From his early years, Andrei went to church with his mother, said his prayers, and believed in God. The Divine Liturgy of the Russian Orthodox, which he experienced, considered that its liturgy transcended time and space. "I remember so well . . . the chanting, the exaltation of worshippers at prayer, the flickering candles, the dark faces of the icons, the radiant mood of my mother and grandmother returning from church after taking communion,"[1] was his vivid recollection. And in the minds of the devout, the liturgy was understood to mirror, exactly, what was happening in heaven simultaneously. Furthermore, all believers around the world, as well as saints and angels, were understood to be participating in this cosmic event, this Divine Liturgy. At some level, did Andrei sense any of this? Was this his introduction to cosmology? It would be irresponsible to say yes. In his writings, he never mentioned the Divine Liturgy. Nevertheless, rituals have an ability to touch deep places in the imagination of a youth and to have a longtime hold on the soul.

At age six, his first tutor, Zinaida, would take him for a walk always to the Cathedral of Christ-the-Savior and, while on the way, she would tell him Bible stories. In his *Memoirs*, he made it a point to mention six other members of his family who fervently believed in God. But at age thirteen he decided that he no longer believed in God, stopped saying his prayers, and attended church only rarely, on special occasions.

On July 10, 1943, when he married Klava Vikhireva, the ceremony did not take place in a church. Actually, her father, according to Andrei, "blessed us with an icon and made the sign of the cross over us, pronouncing some words of guidance. Then, holding hands, the two of us ran across a field to the nearest registry office."[2] That semireligious action was one of the last religious rites of his life. When his daughter, Tanya, was born on February 7, 1945, there was no baptism as far as I can determine. Andrei Sakharov's funeral, on December 18, 1989, took place not in a cathedral but in the Palace of Youth in Moscow. I could not discover if any prayer was said at the service, but it would have been unlikely.

So far, I have only mentioned ritual observances. But what about his musings on the subject of religion? What direct and associated thoughts led to his abrupt and complete separation from religion?

One short answer to that question would have to do with the rise in militant atheism in Russian society at the time of his adolescence, thus positioning religion as a step backward, a regressive step into the contrived mystique of the tsar and the people and the Orthodox faith. In his words, "The oppressiveness, the whole atmosphere of Byzantium, of Russia before Peter the Great—my imagination recoils in horror at seeing the barbarism, lies, and hypocrisy of the past carried into our time."[3] Like so many intellectuals of his age, he happily embraced the social construct of atheism as a liberating and promising way forward. I wish that this former Christian had said more about who Jesus was or wasn't for him. But he wanted the reader to know that he was writing a memoir, not a confession. So at age thirteen, and for many decades to follow, he moved radically from a God-centered universe to a God-absent universe. The atheism of the state had provided a rich opening for an unfettered exploration of scientifically tantalizing mysteries.

Another reason for Sakharov's early rejection of religious faith was the influence of his father, Dmitri. Evidently, Dmitri never broached the subject of religion with his son. Nevertheless, Andrei got the distinct impression that his father had no use for religion. Also, he had the impression that his father wanted Andrei to be the full scientist that Dmitri had wanted to be but had never had the chance to become because of the exigencies of war, revolution, and financial hard times. The fixed divide between science and religion was clear in the mind of the young man as it had been in the mind of his father.

While on the subject of soul-making, I need to mention Andrei's high regard for meticulous and hard work that he observed in his father. Sakharov wrote, "In the 1920s, my father began to write popular scientific works. . . . His writing style was crisp, precise, and lucid, but it cost him a great deal of time and effort. He agonized over every word, and copied sentences again and again in his elegant hand. I used to watch him, and perhaps it was this more than anything else that taught me what it is to truly work."[4] Sakharov's inner constitution was not captured by soft thoughts of heaven but by constant, arduous work on earth.

Regarding another leading influence on his early life, I need to draw attention to his paternal grandmother, Maria Domukhovsky. When she died, Sakharov said, "With her death, the soul seemed to depart from the [Sakharov] house on Granatny Lane [Moscow]."[5] Whatever Sakharov understood as "soul," it was defined by the life and leanings of his grandmother.

Who was this lady who infused the Sakharov home with "soul"? And what did Andrei mean by "soul"? Some day he would apply this sense of "soul" to thermonuclear devices and to human rights advocacy. So these are not idle questions. The few clues that we have drive us back to his grandmother.

Maria Domukhovsky (Maria Petrovna) came from old Russian nobility. In her student days, she fled a six-month marriage and ended up in St. Petersburg rooming with a friend, a "Narodnaya Volya" terrorist, who was arrested and exiled. Maria broke from her noble background, campaigned for personal freedom, and was highly critical of her society. So independent was she that she had six children by Andrei's grandfather, Ivan, before she married him in 1899. As a member of the Russian intelligentsia, she not only became an activist against the injustices of tsarist Russia, but she "collected money for exiles, sent them packages and visited them in prison."[6] Since this was a period of open borders in Russia, she and the family visited France, Italy, Switzerland, and Germany two or three times a year. Then, almost out of the blue, Maria became a devout Christian. All of the above created a marvelously complex and compassionate person.

So here was Maria Petrovna, a mixture of contradictions. Of noble blood, she championed the downtrodden. Thoroughly Russian but emphatically European in culture. Once completely indifferent to pious customs but, in time, mesmerized before icons. Politically active, yet a stay-at-home mother. She had soul, according to young Andrei. She seemed to reach out and embrace all of the major strands of Russian life and hold them to herself, in herself. Her life was Russian life in its fullness, and hers was the soul of Russia. And she lived at Granatny Lane, Moscow, with young Andrei and his family.

Her way of transferring her values and textured opinions to her grandson came through reading to him a great number of books that she loved. As might be expected, there was the poetry of Aleksandr Pushkin—for instance, *The Tale of Tsar Saltan*. He heard the political satire (*Gulliver's Travels*) of Jonathan Swift. Life on the open road in France came through the adventures of a seeming orphan, in Hector Malot's *Sans Famille*. Andrei heard his grandmother read words about slavery from Mark Twain's *Huckleberry Finn*. In choosing to support his black friend, Jim, over the dictates of society, Huckleberry exclaimed, "All right then, I'll *go* to hell." Themes of adventure, defiance, elimination of serfdom and slavery, mockery of established buffoons, championing of the underdog, filled Andrei's mind as he listened intently to his grandmother. Cicero supposedly said, "A room without books is like a body without a soul."[7] Maria and her grandson had a room full of books and soul.

But, for me, the most poignant recollection of Maria Petrovna's readings aloud came with a special yearly reading from the Bible. Not from the poetry or the history or the miracles or the mythical stories of the Bible, but from the Passion narrative! It solely told the account of the redemptive suffering of Jesus. He recalled, "During Holy Week, she would read us the Gospels; I remember her getting upset when (my sister) Irina commented, 'How interesting,' in response to Jesus' words, 'Before the cock crows, you will betray me thrice.' We were perfectly well aware that Grandmother wasn't reading us the Bible as entertainment."[8] Maria was inside the story with its cosmic consequence and personal tragedy. For her, no amount of institutional shortcomings of the Church could hide, for a moment, the grandeur and import of her Lord's Passion. Faith wasn't a matter of objective assent for Maria; it was a full-blooded, subjective embrace. In the early hours of March 27, 1941, Maria Petrovna died, and soon thereafter her funeral was held in the Moscow Cathedral. She was gone from the place that knew her so well and, as Andrei wrote, "With her death, the soul seemed to depart from the house on Granatny Lane."[9]

Sakharov: The Glories and Restraints of Atheism

Classic scientists such as Galileo or Copernicus had to struggle mightily to overcome opposition of the Church and eventually to win approval of the Church for their scientific breakthroughs. Not so with Sakharov! He came into the study of physics during a time when there were no religious restraints. Politically sanctioned atheism by the Soviet Union had unlocked the door for him and others to push the boundaries of theoretical and applied physics and thus enhance and glorify the Soviet Union.

The study of mathematics might have been good sport in high school for the brightest students to show off their scholarly acumen. But, when those students were exposed to the possibilities built into the study of physics, many, like Andrei, leapt forward with confidence and abandon. And the rewards had the potential of being exhilarating. Physicist I. I. Rabi described his profession as a physicist as "rockets all the time. The world was aglow."[10] This was borne out in the words of Sakharov when he began work on the hydrogen bomb. He said, "The physics of atomic and thermonuclear explosions is a genuine theoretician's paradise. A thermonuclear reaction—the mysterious source of the energy of sun and stars, the sustenance of life on Earth but also the potential instrument of its destruction—was within my grasp."[11]

His description of what it was like to be Andrei Sakharov and to be doing what he was doing is devoid of religious sentiment. But to a cleric like me, the picture he paints was like the oldest religious story in the Bible, the story of Adam and Eve in paradise with the apple on the forbidden tree; the apple that contained the knowledge of good and evil was dangling within his grasp. Adam, in the garden, might have anticipated Andrei's words in the Installation (the name given to the place they worked), and could have said, "Life or death were within my grasp." I guess what Andrei was saying was that he astonishingly found himself on the most primitive threshold where life or death was dangling, and he sensed that he could almost grasp the power. For Sakharov, was this a God-like moment? A triumph of human progress?

Andrei wasn't pondering religious questions in 1949. He wasn't even asked to take part in the development of a hydrogen bomb. He was ordered to do it. But he was thrilled, nonetheless. And it was not just infatuation with "superb physics (Fermi's comment on the atom bomb program)"[12] that provided his primary motivation. He said, "What was most important for me at the time . . . was the conviction that our work was essential. . . . I understood, of course, the terrifying, inhuman nature of the weapons we were building. But the recent war (WWII) had also been an exercise in barbarity; and . . . I regarded myself as a soldier in this new scientific war . . . the sacrifices that our country has made should not be in vain. . . . We never questioned the vital importance of our work. . . . High salaries, government awards, and other privileges and marks of distinction contributed to the

Andrei Sakharov, Stanford University, 1989. Photo by Harvey Lynch.

psychological atmosphere in which we lived."[13] His motivation, at the very beginning, came from love of country and from self-interest and was void of religious reflections.

In 1949, he was a man of the Soviet Union. Its history of brutally starved, executed, besieged, forgotten, defeated people burned in his heart. If its greatest nuclear adversary, the United States, stood over it with a nuclear threat, Sakharov was only too happy to strive for thermonuclear parity by helping to create the first hydrogen bomb. For him, it was a way forward to assure peace and security for his people. To whom was he ultimately accountable? In 1949, the answer was the Soviet Union.

It is important to note that his allegiance was not to the Communist Party but was, instead, to the Soviet Union. On several occasions, he was strongly encouraged to join the party, but he steadfastly refused, being fully aware of atrocities in the past perpetrated by the party. He particularly deplored the party's arrest and execution of hundreds of thousands of innocent people and the excesses of the collectivization campaign during the Yezhov purges of 1936–1938, called the Great Terror.

Just as Andrei Sakharov came to a moment when he could not anchor his trust in God, even so he later came to a time when he could not anchor his trust in the Soviet Union. Political atheism granted a few freedoms but denied a host of other freedoms. Slowly, Sakharov came to terms with the shortcomings of the system he had served so well. There were a host of turning points, but the most vivid, for me, was when he was being honored for the successful test of the hydrogen bomb.

At the end of the day, November 22, 1955, Marshal Mitrofan Nedelin gave a banquet, and many military and government officials turned out. Andrei was asked to give the first toast. He rose with a glass of brandy in his hand and said something like, "May all our devices explode as successfully as today's, but always over test sites and never over cities."[14]

He said, "The table fell silent, as if I had said something indecent."[15] Quickly, Marshal Nedelin rose and said, "Let me tell a parable. An old man wearing only a shirt was praying before an icon. 'Guide me, harden me. Guide me, harden me.' His wife, who was lying on the stove, said, 'Just pray to be hard, old man, I can guide it in myself.'"[16]

Andrei later said, "Many years have passed, but I still feel as if I had been lashed by a whip. Not that my feelings were hurt; I am not easily offended, especially by a joke. But Nedelin's parable was not a joke. He wanted to squelch my pacifist sentiment, and to put me and anyone who might share these ideas in our place. The point of the story (half-lewd, half blasphemous, which added to its unpleasant effect) was clear enough. We, the inventors, scientists, engineers, craftsmen, had created a terrible weapon, the most terrible weapon in human history; but its use would lie entirely out of our control. The people at the top of the Party and military hierarchy would make the decisions. Of course, I knew this already—I wasn't naïve. But understanding something in an abstract way is different from feeling it with your whole being, like the reality of life and death. The ideas and emotions kindled at that moment have not diminished to this day, and they completely altered my thinking."[17]

Two words jump out at me in his comments. One is *blasphemous*. And one is *naïve*.

Blasphemy, or showing contempt for sacred things, is a strange word for a man who didn't believe in God and who lived in an atheistic state. It raises the question: what exactly was sacred for him in his country? Later on, in his Nobel Prize speech, he did answer that question. He passionately stated that "our sacred endeavors in this world of ours"[18] should not be minimized. He went on to say, "We must make good the demands of reason and create a life worthy of ourselves and of the goals that we only dimly perceive."[19] In 1955, Sakharov would gradually leave the privileged class and find himself, more and more, in league with the humiliated and voiceless class.

On that night in 1955, Andrei appeared to be naïve. That is exactly the word that always is at the heart of nuclear debate. The realists talk about the need for a vastly superior war chest of nuclear arms and refer to those calling for abolition as "nuclear naïve." On the other hand, the abolitionists see the realists as "nuclear naïve" about human nature, motives, and capacity for perfection in policing weapons. "I wasn't *that* naïve,"[20] says Sakharov. But aren't we all? The ground can't hold our nuclear waste. The number of nations and rogue groups wanting the weapons keeps growing. The price of creating and modernizing the weapons pushes ordinary life issues off the table and threatens financial bankruptcy for all possessors of nuclear weapons. And, short of a catastrophic nuclear moment, no leading nuclear country can harness sufficient political will among its citizens to make a profound change of direction. We don't rule the weapons; they rule us. Naïve? Aren't we all?

I realize that I am in danger of making too much of the night of November 22, 1955. But nevertheless, there is one more thing for me and that is the contrast between Robert Oppenheimer and Andrei Sakharov on the nights when each had a successful breakthrough test. On July 16, 1945, near Alamogordo, New Mexico, Oppenheimer was in charge of the first artificial nuclear explosion in a spot that he code-named Trinity. This Jewish scientist chose a very religious word, *Trinity*, saying that he took inspiration from one of John Donne's "Holy Sonnets." Perhaps it was the Fourteenth Sonnet, which begins with these words: "Batter my heart, three person'd God."

Later on, Oppenheimer said that two sections of the *Bhagavad Gita* ran through his mind after the success of the atomic test. First, "If the radiance of a thousand suns were to burst at once into the sky, that would be like the splendor of the mighty one."[21] Second, Oppenheimer quoted from chapter 11, verses 31–33, which tells about the epic battle of Mahabharata, in which Prince Arjuna hesitates to attack the enemy with his army. Vishnu, the incarnation of Krishna (the Supreme God), encourages Arjuna to unleash his might. Overwhelmed, Arjuna asks Vishnu, "Tell me who are You in such a fierce form?" To which the Supreme Lord says, "I am death, the mighty destroyer of the world, out to destroy. . . . Conquer your enemies and enjoy a prosperous kingdom. All these (opposing warriors) have already been destroyed by Me. You are only an instrument, O Arjuna."[22]

If the mind of Robert Oppenheimer swirled with religious imagery on the night of his big breakthrough, the mind of Andrei Sakharov was devoid of religious associations and singularly occupied by lessons in the fundamental power dynamics of an atheistic political order. In both cases, the men were profoundly disquieted by what they had helped to create, and both men would be forever haunted about what they had done.

Sakharov: Long on Human Rights, Short of Heaven's Reach

Although the soul seemed to go out of his home in Moscow in 1941, the soul of Andrei Sakharov was much in evidence all the days of his mature life. And just because he stopped believing in God at age thirteen didn't mean that he did not have second thoughts. I want to address both of these suppositions.

Soul Expressed Emphatically in Terms of Human Rights Advocacy

Sakharov did not come to advocacy of conscience trusting the positive affirmations of the Bill of Rights of the United States of America and a Creator who bequeathed "certain unalienable rights." Nor did he come armed with Mahatma Gandhi's negatively stated dangers to human virtue: "Wealth without work, pleasure without conscience, knowledge without character, business without ethics, science without humanity, religion without sacrifice, politics without principle."[23] He ascended this road by experiencing, himself, the full brunt of a totalitarian system that was determined to silence him and to mute his powerful voice of advocacy. And this persecution led him inexorably into championing the human rights of other scholars and friends. This life of the soul was what was ultimately at stake for Sakharov.

In his Nobel Prize speech, read by his wife, Elena Bonner Sakharov, he wrote, "It is unbearable to consider that at this very moment (December 11, 1975) that we are gathered together in this hall on this festive occasion, hundreds and thousands of prisoners of conscience are suffering from undernourishment. . . . They shiver with cold, damp, and exhaustion in ill-lit dungeons, where they are forced to wage a ceaseless struggle for their human dignity and their conviction against the 'indoctrination machine,' in fact against the very destruction of their souls."[24]

What a partner in advocacy was Elena Bonner Sakharov! She was indefatigable in her efforts. Together they took every spare moment to visit prisoners in jail or to appear in court or to write supportive letters to government officials. The part of his Nobel Prize speech, which she delivered on his behalf, the part that touched me most deeply, was when he paused to mention, by name, 114 prison internees known to him personally. And to mention three, by name, who were in exile. And three more, by name, who were awaiting verdicts. No pious person at prayer with an intercession list ever prayed more muscularly!

He wanted to share his prize with these remembered prisoners of conscience. Furthermore, he said, "I should like all those whose names I have not mentioned to forgive me. Every single name, mentioned as well as unmentioned, represents a hard and heroic human destiny, years of suffering, years of struggling for human dignity."[25] From there, his imagination and resolve for human rights extended from the Soviet Union to all countries as well as the universe itself. Since he postulated the existence of planets similar to ours and beings similar to us in the universe, a high regard for human rights would be universal and boundless.

Belief in God Seriously Revisited

In 1958, Joshua Lederberg won the Nobel Prize in Physiology or Medicine and moved to Stanford University. He said, "A religious impulse guides our motives in sustaining scientific enquiry."[26] And here I am fifty-six years later at Stanford trying to imagine, on one level, what role motives play in Sakharov's scientific inquiry and, on another level, wondering if there is such a thing as "religious impulse" standing behind and guiding his motives.

In a statement that reflected his doctrine of the worth of human life and capacity for creative thought, Sakharov said, "We must make good the demands of reason and create a life worthy of ourselves and of the goals we only dimly perceive."[27] Did a religious impulse stand behind his motive? Clearly, he would not have claimed that to be true, although every major religion in the world would have deemed his actions to be deeply religious in nature.

The question then arises for me as to whether or not motives have any standing in scientific enquiry. One of the letters that went out for this conference stated, "Scientific research is an adventure of discovery by the human mind over uncharted seas toward the distant, endless frontiers of nature. As such, it is intrinsically amoral." That sentence snapped my head backward. If that is so, then why not permit North Korean and Iranian scientists to exercise their adventure of discovery in scientific research? But motives do matter, it seems to me, even in science. Otherwise, scientists are moral virgins and ethical eunuchs, sort of beyond accountability.

At the end of 1962, the Soviet Union planned a large nuclear test, a test that would harm hundreds of thousands of people not only through radiation, but by non-threshold biological effects such as carcinogenesis and genetic change. Sakharov appealed even to Nikita Khrushchev to delay the test. But to no avail. Sakharov wrote, "It was the ultimate defeat for me. A terrible crime was about to be committed, and I could do nothing to prevent it. I was overcome by my impotence, unbearable bitterness, shame, and humiliation. I put my face down on my desk and wept."[28] To me, this was not the picture of a scientist on an amoral adventure of discovery.

Did a religious impulse guide the motives of Andrei Sakharov? Clearly, the church of his youth, the Russian Orthodox Church, repulsed him. Later on in life he said, "I dislike official churches, especially those closely tied to the state, those of a predominately ceremonial character, or those tainted by fanaticism and intolerance."[29] Yet, after supporting the rights of Seventh-Day Adventists, he could say that he found them to be "pure, sincere, inspired folks."[30] He found the same among faithful Baptists, Catholics, Orthodox, and Muslims. Despite witnessing numerous occasions of hypocrisy and bigotry, he admitted, "On the whole, I have nothing but admiration for those who are sincerely religious."[31]

Religion is one thing. God is something else. Although Sakharov sometimes wrote about religion, as far as I could tell he never used the word *God*. The closest that he came was when he was writing about standard cosmology and the inevitable problem comes up as to what existed before the first cycle of expansion. Was there a divine being behind the act of creation? Sakharov dismissed the question entirely by saying, "The basic religious concept of the divine meaning of existence does not concern science and lies·beyond its limits."[32] So, he was not debunking the assumption of a supreme being, not like Toto in Oz pulling back the curtain and exposing an old, wrinkled man. For Sakharov, an impenetrable wall separated the pursuit of science on the one side and the domain of the divine (not his words) on the other. His heart and soul were invested entirely on one side of the wall. Almost!

In a statement that seems to come from left field, Sakharov states, "I am unable to imagine the universe and human life without some guiding principle, without a source of spiritual 'warmth' that is nonmaterial and not bound by physical laws. Probably this sense of things could be called 'religion.'"[33] He takes great pains not to use the word *God,* but instead substitutes words like *principle* and *religion* and *spiritual warmth* to keep him anchored in the human dimension, help him avoid cheap God-talk, but still point outward and higher. I think that he found himself where the vaguely deist founders of the American democracy found themselves—that is, wanting to hint that something greater stands beyond us and guides us, but as to who or what that is and how that happens, they would rather not speculate. Out of respect and humility, not out of disregard!

In my mind, there is little difference between the statement by Lederberg and the statement by Sakharov. Joshua Lederberg said, "A religious impulse guides our motives in sustaining scientific enquiry." Andrei Sakharov said, "I am unable to imagine the universe and human life without some guiding principle, without a source of spiritual 'warmth' that is nonmaterial and not bound by physical laws."

Summary

What intrigued me most as I started an investigation into the life of Andrei Sakharov was his unofficial title of "Father of the Hydrogen Bomb." It might not have been entirely fair to label him as such because he did not work alone; an entire team of experts was needed. He probably disliked the title. Nevertheless, the title stuck. And I wondered, what went on in the mind and heart of this man who was referred to as the Father of the Hydrogen Bomb? For this he was privileged, but also he had to wear a scarlet *H* on his sweater. How did the prospect of being the author of unspeakable horror sit with him? What inward resources did he call upon to carry this burden? In short, what sort of soul did he possess, given that title?

At the completion of my exploration, I end up with the impression that he was a man of monumental ambiguity, ambiguity of biblical proportions.

In the arena of human rights, a case can be made that he was clearly a world leader in advocacy and impact. On the other hand, if the hydrogen bomb that he "fathered" were detonated in battle and other such weapons, in turn, were detonated in battle, he would be an accomplice to trumping the original Big Bang with a final destructive Big Bang. What good are human rights when there are no humans?

In the arena of religion, his remarks about faith bring to my mind the picture of Jacob wrestling with God.

> Jacob was left alone; and a man wrestled with him until daybreak. When the man saw that he did not prevail against Jacob, he struck him on the hip socket; and Jacob's hip was put out of joint as he wrestled with him. Then he said, "Let me go, for the day is breaking." But Jacob said, "I will not let you go, unless you bless me." So he said to him, "What is your name?" And he said, "Jacob." Then the man said, "You shall no longer be called Jacob, but Israel, for you have striven with God and with humans, and have prevailed." Then Jacob asked him, "Please tell me your name." But he said, "Why is it that you ask my name?" And there he blessed him. So Jacob called the place Peniel, saying "For I have seen God face to face, and yet my life is preserved." The sun rose upon him as he passed Peniel, limping because of his hip.[34]

From my faraway and feeble perspective, Andrei Sakharov appears to be someone who caught a glimpse of the alpha and omega, who believed in the sacred dimension of human life and its potential for progress, and who walked with a biblical limp.

Finally, I would like to thank Sidney Drell and George Shultz for the honor of being here and for the terror of writing for you all and for speaking here. It afforded me an opportunity of getting acquainted with a great man whose nobility of character deserves generations of attention.

In the game of baseball, the job of a leadoff hitter is simply to get on first base. Bunt, walk, get hit by the pitch, scratch out an infield single. Just get on base because the big hitters will be following you. I truly am looking forward to the cleanup hitters here who actually knew Andrei Sakharov, worked with him, studied him, and shared critical moments of history with him. I thank you all.

Notes

1. Andrei Sakharov, *Memoirs* (New York: Alfred A. Knopf, 1990), 4.
2. Ibid., 57.
3. Ibid., 5.
4. Ibid., 13.
5. Ibid., 38.
6. Richard Lourie, *Sakharov: A Biography* (Lebanon, NH: University Press of New England, 2002), 8.
7. Attributed to Marcus Tullius Cicero, Roman author, orator, and politician (106 BC–43 BC).
8. Sakharov, *Memoirs*, 11.
9. Ibid., 38.
10. Lourie, *Sakharov*, 40.
11. Sakharov, *Memoirs*, 96.
12. Lourie, *Sakharov*, 96.
13. Sakharov, *Memoirs*, 97, 116.
14. Ibid., 194.
15. Ibid.
16. Ibid.
17. Ibid.
18. Andrei Sakharov, "Peace, Progress, Human Rights," Nobel Lecture (read by Elena Bonner), December 11, 1975, published in *Nobel Lectures, Peace 1971–1980* (Singapore: World Scientific Publishing, 1997), http://www.nobelprize.org/nobel_prizes/peace/laureates/1975/sakharov-lecture.html.
19. Ibid.
20. Sakharov, *Memoirs*, 195.
21. *Bhagavad Gita*, XI, 12, Translated by Ramanand Prasad (Fremont, CA: American Gita Society, 1995), 181.
22. Ibid., XI, 31–33.
23. *The Collected Works of Mahatma Gandhi* (electronic edition), vol. 33, 133–34.
24. Sakharov, "Peace, Progress, Human Rights," 7.
25. Ibid.
26. Henry Margenau and Roy A. Varghese, eds., *Cosmos, Bios, Theos: Scientists Reflect on Science, God, and the Origins of the Universe, Life and Homo Sapiens* (Peru, IL: Open Court Publishing, 1992), 184.

27. Sakharov, "Peace, Progress, Human Rights," 8.

28. Sakharov, *Memoirs*, 229.

29. Ibid., 4.

30. Ibid., 5.

31. Ibid.

32. Ibid., 543.

33. Ibid., 4.

34. Sakharov, *Memoirs*, 4.

Environmental Effects
of Nuclear War

Raymond Jeanloz

> The salvation of our environment requires that we overcome our divisions and the pressure of temporary, local interests.
>
> —Andrei Sakharov, *Progress, Coexistence, and Intellectual Freedom* (1968)

In his 1975 Nobel lecture, Andrei Sakharov linked preservation of the environment to arms control, human rights, and global progress. Here I turn to a specific aspect of this linkage: the possibility that even a limited use of nuclear weapons in one region of the world could have significant environmental consequences around the globe. If true, this would amount to regional nuclear war victimizing much of the human population as innocent bystanders, reinforcing the understanding that use of nuclear weapons would be catastrophic.

At a time when blast and radiation were the focus of discussions regarding the effects of nuclear weapons (e.g., Glasstone and Dolan 1977), work by Paul Crutzen, Richard Turco, and colleagues brought attention to the broader environmental consequences of nuclear war (Crutzen and Birks 1982; Turco et al.

I thank J. F. Ahearne, W. F. Burns, P. R. Buseck, C. F. Chyba, S. D. Drell, L. Eden, J. O. Ellis, I. Y. Fung, R. L. Garwin, T. M. Hardebeck, D. J. Holloway, M. D. Lowenthal, W. J. Perry, A. Robock, C. W. Stubbs, O. B. Toon, and R. P. Turco for helpful discussions and comments. I also thank the Hoover Institution at Stanford University for its hospitality and support of this work. All listed web sites were accessed January 24, 2015.

1983, 1990; Crutzen 1984; Crutzen et al. 1984; Thompson et al. 1984; Small and Bush 1985; Malone et al. 1986; Small 1989; Robock et al. 2007a). In particular, they proposed that fires ignited by nuclear explosions in a massive exchange between the United States and the Soviet Union would produce enough soot to significantly modify the atmosphere, leading to worldwide cooling ("nuclear winter") that could drastically affect the global population, including in nations that had not participated in the war. Food supplies would be greatly reduced, for instance, because of shortened growing seasons and harsher conditions over several years' duration.

Although early work on nuclear winter focused on large-scale war, with explosions totaling yields of one thousand to five thousand megatons (i.e., one to five billion tons of TNT-equivalent energy release), more recent studies have emphasized the consequences of much smaller regional nuclear exchanges having a combined explosion yield of one to two megatons. Specifically, a total of one hundred Hiroshima-scale (fifteen-kiloton) explosions have been suggested as potentially representative of a regional nuclear war affecting the atmosphere for several years (Toon et al. 2007; Robock et al. 2007b; Mills et al. 2008, 2014). Whether these scenarios are representative or not, thankfully, amounts to speculation. Still, the results of these studies can be effectively scaled so that the findings could be applied to alternative scenarios.

Two primary questions are: (1) how much soot would be lofted into the atmosphere during a nuclear war? and (2) what is the impact on the human population of a given amount of soot in the atmosphere? The focus here is on changes in surface temperature and precipitation, but many additional effects should be taken into account, from depletion of ozone in the atmosphere to the spread of radioactive fallout. The longer-term consequences of climate change, such as food shortages, are not considered here in any detail, though they could ultimately be more severe in terms of death, disease, and injury than the immediate consequences of the nuclear explosions. Similarly, loss of infrastructure is not discussed.

Amount of Soot Lofted into the Atmosphere

Toon et al. (2007) describe an approach to estimating the amount of soot generated by fires caused by a regional nuclear exchange, considering thirteen nations as possible targets. The assumptions are spelled out in the paper, so they can be analyzed or modified in order to evaluate alternative scenarios. For example, the authors consider soot to have the optical properties of black carbon without organic compounds (see the following for a discussion of the nature of soot and black carbon: Pósfai and Buseck 2010; Bond et al. 2013; Buseck et al. 2014).[1] Overall, the results of Toon and colleagues suggest that about two megatons (2 trillion grams) of soot can be lofted into the atmosphere per one megaton total explosion yield (figure 4.1).[2] The distribution appears skewed, with notable instances producing

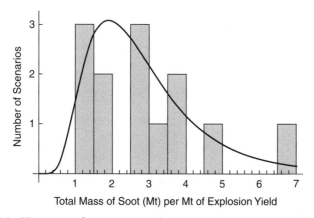

Figure 4.1. Histogram of scenarios considered by O. B. Toon et al., summarizing the amount of soot lofted into the atmosphere per one megaton total explosive yield that they calculate for regional nuclear exchanges. They assume that fuel loading (figure 2) is proportional to population density, and that targeting would proceed from densest to less-dense population centers; hence the distribution shown here reflects the sizes and densities of population centers considered. The calculations are for a total of fifty fifteen-kiloton explosions (0.75 megaton total yield) in each of two nations, giving a total explosion-energy release of 1.5 megatons. The typical amount of atmospheric soot for these scenarios would be near three megatons (equaling a 1.5 megaton yield times the peak value of two megatons of soot per megaton of yield), and extends beyond six to ten megatons (e.g., for India and China; lognormal distribution illustrated by *curve*).

two to three times this amount of soot, depending on the scenario considered. In particular, nuclear explosions over densely populated urban areas in the tropics are found to have the greatest consequences.

There are many uncertainties in such an analysis, the greatest no doubt being the individual locations and sizes of nuclear explosions relative to population density (or fuel loading) that should be considered representative of a regional war (Dolan 1972, 3-1–3-113 and 9-13–9-67; articles by Carrier et al. (1984, 1985) and Pitts (1991); and chapters by Postol (15–72) and Brode and Small (73–95) in NRC (1986) describe the nature of urban firestorms most likely to produce significant amounts of soot; also Eden 2006, 221–82).[3] The estimated soot production is tightly correlated with fuel loading, the mass per unit area of material consumed by fires (figure 4.2).

The typical case considered by Toon and colleagues (e.g., 2008; see also Stenke et al. 2013) has a population density of 20,000 people per square kilometer, with eleven tons of fuel per person and a soot emission factor of 1.6 percent (i.e., 16 kilograms of soot generated per ton of fuel burned).[4] This gives 3,520 tons per square kilometer of soot production, or about forty-six thousand tons per explosion, assuming thirteen square kilometers of burnt area per explosion based on the experience of Hiroshima; one hundred Hiroshima-scale explosions (fifteen kilotons yield each) then result in 4.6 megatons of soot put into the atmosphere, or about three megatons per megaton of total explosive yield. The implied fuel loading of 220 kilograms per square meter is in line with Toon et al.'s (2007) range of estimates for individual countries (figure 4.2).[5]

One of the important developments bearing on fuel loading is the emergence of megacities over recent decades. In 2014, these large, densely populated urban centers contained about 7 percent of the global population, which itself is more than 50 percent urbanized.[6] The increase in population density over time, because of growth in global population and because of its increased spatial concentration, means that nuclear explosions have potentially larger consequences than ever before. Numerous military, indus-

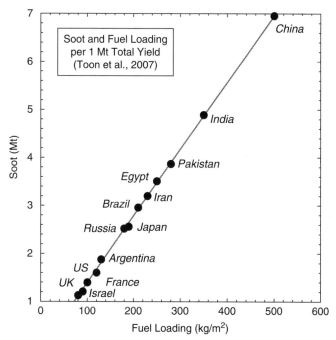

Figure 4.2. Amount of soot (black carbon) lofted into the atmosphere as a function of fuel loading (mass per unit area of material consumed by fire) for regional nuclear exchanges, as calculated by Toon et al. (2007). The amount of soot is normalized per one megaton total explosive yield, as in figure 4.1 that gives a histogram for the group of target nations shown here (for each nation, targeting is assumed to proceed from densest to less-dense population centers: see figures 6 and 12 of Toon et al. 2007).

trial, and communications centers are in or near urban areas, as are many sites for command and control. Therefore, even a small initial nuclear exchange in a zone of active battle could plausibly expand to the level of soot production considered by Toon et al. (2007) for a regional war.

These qualitative arguments, on top of their specific numerical estimates, led Toon and coworkers to conclude that about five megatons of soot (black carbon) injection into the atmosphere must realistically be considered a potential outcome of a limited nuclear exchange. As they point out, independent estimates should be made under alternative assumptions in order to better understand the range and uncertainties of soot that would likely be produced by nuclear war.

Environmental Impact of Atmospheric Soot

The consequences of a given amount of soot being put into the atmosphere are large, and are relatively well-determined. Because of its darkness (high absorption of visible light), black carbon is the second most important atmospheric constituent controlling climate change (Bond and Bergstrom 2006; Bond et al. 2013). Most is normally present in the dense lower atmosphere, where it has a residence time of about one week (five to fifteen days) (Chin et al. 2009). With a median input rate of about eight to ten megatons per year, this amounts to a steady-state background of approximately 0.2–0.4 megatons of soot being present in the atmosphere (cf. Pósfai and Buseck 2010, table 2).

In comparison, injection of one to five megatons of soot as a result of nuclear explosions causes a significant perturbation to the atmosphere, due to the rapid emplacement of approximately five to twenty-five times the normal background amount of soot. Calculations by Robock et al. (2007b) and Mills et al. (2008, 2014) confirm this impression in terms of climate impact, as they find maximum drops in global mean surface temperature and precipitation of about 0.25–1.5°C (0.5–2.7°F) and 0.05–0.2 millimeters per day (2–7 percent), respectively (figure 4.3a). For comparison, Northern Hemisphere surface temperature was about 0.5°C cooler during the Little Ice Age of the sixteenth to eighteenth centuries than in the mid-twentieth century.

It is not just the magnitude but also the duration of these effects that is important, with anomalously cool, dry, and ozone-depleted conditions being predicted to last five to ten years or more in response to a five-megaton soot injection into the atmosphere (Mills et al. 2008, 2014). Mean global ocean temperature is similarly calculated to drop for more than a decade to at least 200 meters depth.

A key reason for this long-lasting effect is that a large fraction of the soot is lofted by solar heating of the black-carbon-loaded air into the stratosphere, where the soot can be widely distributed around the globe and is not subject to raining out as in the lower atmosphere. The process is well understood, with initial injection of nuclear explosion-produced soot going through the top of the troposphere (lower atmosphere) (e.g., NRC 1986, 28–38 and 91–94; Utyuzhnikov 2013). The large concentration of soot initially present at the top of the troposphere absorbs incoming sunlight, thereby warming the surrounding air that then rises and lifts the included soot well into the stratosphere.

It is this extra lifting that makes the soot from nuclear-explosion firestorms both long-lasting and potent in its effects, with the stratosphere being warmed by 50 degrees Celsius or more for a five-megaton source of black carbon (e.g., Mills et al. 2014). The lifting also causes the surface temperature to cool due to absorption of incoming sunlight that now does not make it to the ground. In contrast, soot normally contributes to global *warming*, as it is present in the lower atmosphere where it warms the surrounding air (Bond et al. 2013). Heating of the stratosphere in the nuclear-war scenario greatly increases the rate at which ozone is destroyed, with detrimental effects on agriculture and human health due to more of the sun's ultraviolet radiation reaching Earth's surface.

There are several ways of checking these calculations. For example, Stenke et al. (2013) carried out independent climate simulations for a five-megaton soot injection into the atmosphere. Using a separate set of general-circulation models for the atmosphere and coupled ocean interactions, they found similar results to those of Robock et al. (2007b) (figure 4.3a). There are differences in assumptions, including how the oceans are treated and how the optical properties of soot are modeled; both sets of calculations can be considered representative of the state of the art in current climate simulations (Mills et al. 2014).

A second check is to compare with the effects of natural events, of which the 1991 Mount Pinatubo eruption is perhaps the best example because of its magnitude and the fact that its effects were relatively well documented by satellite and other observations (e.g., Soden et al. 2002). However, the eruption injected sulfate and mineral aerosols into the stratosphere, not the highly absorptive black carbon. Therefore, I use the decrease in short-wavelength radiation reaching Earth's surface to identify the

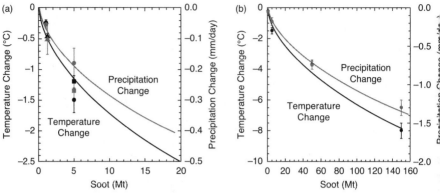

Figure 4.3. Maximum change in global mean surface temperature (*black curve, scale on left*) and precipitation (*gray curve, scale on right*) as a function of the total amount of soot lofted into the atmosphere due to nuclear explosions, as calculated (*filled circles*) by Robock et al. (2007a, b) and Mills et al. (2014) for regional (*a*) and global war (*b*). Global mean precipitation is 3 mm/day in these models. Stenke et al.'s (2013) calculations for 5 Mt soot are shown for comparison in (*a*) (*squares*), as are the temperature and precipitation anomalies observed as a result of the 1991 Mount Pinatubo eruption (*a*) (*triangles* at 1.2 Mt soot): an equivalent soot release was derived by matching the drop in short-wave radiation observed and modeled for the natural event with calculations for the eruption and for nuclear explosions (Robock et al., 2007b), using the temperature anomaly from Soden et al. (2002) and precipitation scaled from Trenberth and Dai (2007).

equivalent atmospheric soot loading for the eruption (1.2 ± 0.3 megatons), and find good agreement with the model calculations for surface temperature and precipitation anomalies due to nuclear explosion-induced soot (figure 4.3a). Though at the low end of nuclear scenarios considered here, the Pinatubo event was the largest volcanic eruption of the twentieth century, and it caused measurable changes in surface temperature and precipitation. Future observations of similar—or perhaps even smaller—natural events may significantly improve empirical validation of the models shown in figure 4.3.

A third check on these models is to investigate the specific processes involved, such as the "self-lifting" of soot into the stratosphere (i.e., by warming the atmosphere in which the soot resides). The idea was proposed early in the study of nuclear winter (Crutzen and Birks 1982), but the spatial-temporal pervasiveness, resolution, and diversity of modern Earth observations now allow direct observation of this phenomenon. For example, satellite imagery of the 2009 Australian Black Saturday smoke plume shows strong indications of this self-lifting process, with the plume having reached 20 kilometers altitude—well into the stratosphere—within days and then circling the globe over six to eight weeks before dissipating (Siddaway and Petelina 2011; de Laat et al. 2012).

Discussion and Conclusions

Despite nuclear winter having been considered controversial and poorly constrained when it was first discussed, the controversy ultimately was less about the substantive scientific findings than about how to present the results to policymakers and the public at large (e.g., NRC 1985; Sagan et al. 1986; Marshall 1987; Carrier 1990; Turco et al. 1991; Eden 2006, 238–242; Oreskes and Conway 2011, 47–54 and 59–64). Key technical aspects of the proposed atmospheric effects have been confirmed through improved calculations and field observations over the past two to three decades; modern estimates of environmental impact due to large-scale nuclear war (figure 4.3b), which are far more extensive than previously possible, are in broad agreement with the earlier findings (Robock et al. 2007a; Toon et al. 2008).

Overall, observations and calculations support the conclusion that injection of three to five megatons of soot high into the atmosphere can have significant, detrimental effects on the global human population. This result needs to be better documented and better understood, especially through improved observations of the Earth and its atmosphere, but the perturbation is large in comparison with the background amount (and flux) of soot in the atmosphere.

The present discussion offers but a crude summary of the modeled consequences of atmospheric soot loading due to nuclear conflict. The climate simulations show that the effects vary considerably both in space and time, for instance, with global cooling being systematically more intense over land than the oceans. The impact on food production is thereby heightened (in comparison with merely considering global averages), and analyses of the consequences of a regional nuclear exchange in South Asia reveal significant reductions in agricultural production in East Asia and North America (Özdogan et al. 2013; Xia and Robock 2013). For this war scenario with a five-megaton soot injection, Mills et al. (2014) derive a five-year seasonal average shortfall in precipitation of 60–80 percent across the Middle East and in parts of South America, with a corresponding reduction in the frost-free growing season of twenty days or more across much of Northern Europe, North Africa, and the upper Midwest of North America.

These and many other effects remain to be explored in greater detail. However, the more significant uncertainties lie in the underlying scenarios, because it does little good to policymakers to conclude that, say, a three- to five-megaton soot injection into the atmosphere is unacceptable. If, for instance, it is confirmed that as little as a few megatons of total nuclear-explosion yield can cause unacceptable environmental damage, this has significant consequences for policymakers, whether in the United States or elsewhere. Therefore, it is important to establish the reliability of this conclusion for each given scenario of nuclear explosions, and how much it might change for alternative (plausible) scenarios.

The details matter, as illustrated by the dozen atmospheric tests with explosive yields over ten megatons that did not loft megatons of soot into the atmosphere.[7] Because they were conducted in the Marshall Islands and Novaya Zemlya, these tests did not generate the large fires expected—in many instances—from military use of nuclear weapons, as considered in the nuclear-winter scenarios (e.g., NRC 1986, 81). It is for this reason that detailed scenarios—the individual locations and sizes of nuclear explosions relative to fuel loading—need to be specifically considered in evaluating the environmental consequences of nuclear war. It is important to note that there may be systematic differences between the conclusions of military planners who consider the sizes and locations of explosions causing a certain level of *assured* damage, and researchers evaluating the *possible* range of environmental consequences for a given scenario (e.g., OTA 1979, 3; NRC 1986, 86; Eden 2006, 38–49, 221–282).

Some experts may argue that use of nuclear weapons is so devastating and unpredictable that there is little point to considering the environmental consequences of nuclear war. That argument is too facile, however, in that there would, no doubt, be many survivors of a regional nuclear war, yet those survivors could be subjected to terrible longer-term consequences of the detonations. Whether bystanders or engaged in the conflict, nations need to be cognizant of these consequences beforehand.

In conclusion, the work done to date establishes that there is a significant issue to be addressed in realistically evaluating the environmental impact of nuclear war, even for a regional conflict. Far more sophisticated climate simulations are now carried out than were previously possible, and—at least as important—the potential climate response to soot loading can be documented through the vastly more reliable, pervasive, and diverse observations currently being made of Earth's atmosphere, oceans, and land masses. There are no bystanders likely to remain unaffected by nuclear conflict of any scale, and the consequences can be far worse than a simple quantification of explosive yield might imply. The governments of the major powers have the scientific resources to investigate the potential impacts of explosions from a few dozen modest-yield nuclear weapons being used anywhere around the world, and therefore have a responsibility to do so.

Notes

1. The fluffy, nonspherical shape of the aggregated particles and the optical properties of the individual carbon nanospheres both contribute to the high absorption of visible light by the soot.

2. Note that megaton is used both as a unit of explosive yield (energy released by one million tons of TNT) and as a unit of mass for soot. Though potentially confusing, this gives the mnemonic that one megaton yield from nuclear explosions can produce on the order of one megaton soot from the resulting fires.

3. Detonations are assumed to be above the "fallout-free" height of burst in the present discussion, whereas explosions at lower altitude create

significant additional harm due to radioactive fallout (e.g., NRC 2005; Jeanloz 2012).

4. There are more than thirty cities worldwide with a population density exceeding 20,000 people per square kilometer, the densest being Manila (43,000 people/km^2); more than forty-five city districts exceed 50,000 people/km^2 (peaking at 130,000–170,000 people/km^2 in Dhaka); more than forty-five zip codes in the United States have population densities above 20,000 people/km^2 (peaking at close to 40,000–60,000 people/km^2 in Manhattan). See http://en.wikipedia. org/wiki/List_of_cities_proper_by_population_density, http://en .wikipedia.org/wiki/List_of_city_districts_by_population_density, and http://zipatlas.com/us/zip-code-comparison/population-density.htm.

5. For comparison, table 8.1 of Chandler et al. (1983) (also given by Rehm et al. 2002) lists urban fuel loads of 20–50 kg/m^2 for dwellings, offices, and schools (excluding archives, libraries, etc.); 40 kg/m^2 times the number of floors for apartments; 50–100 kg/m^2 for shops; and 30–300 kg/m^2 or more for industrial and storage sites. From their studies of US cities, Bush et al. (1991) found fuel loads of 134–225 kg/m^2 per covered area of residential to industrial settings, with coverage of 10–22 percent resulting in average loads of 13–44 kg/m^2 (see also Culver 1978 and chapter 5 of section 12 in NFPA 2003). Extrapolating to dense megacities outside the United States is likely to increase these values. In addition, there are indications that changes in construction materials and building contents have increased fuel loads over time (e.g., Kerber 2012), whereas establishment and improved enforcement of fire codes can serve to limit or decrease fuel loads over time.

6. http://www.megacities.uni-koeln.de/index.htm.

7. See http://en.wikipedia.org/wiki/List_of_nuclear_weapons _tests.

References

Bond, T. C., and R. W. Bergstrom. 2006. "Light Absorption by Carbonaceous Particles: An Investigative Review." *Aerosol Science and Technology* 40, no. 1: 26–67.

Bond, T. C., S. J. Dherty, D. W. Fahey, P. M. Forster, T. Bernsten, B. J. DeAngelo, M. G. Flanner, S. Ghan, B. Kärcher, D. Koch, S. Kinne, Y. Kondo, P. K. Quinn, M. C. Sarofim, M.G. Schultz, C. Venkataraman, H. Zhang, S. Zhang, N. Bellouin, S. K. Guttikunda, P. K. Hopke, M. Z. Jacobson, J. W. Kaiser, Z. Klimont, U. Lohmann, J. P. Schwarz, D. Shindell, T. Storelvmo, S. G. Warren, and

C. S. Zender. 2013. "Bounding the Role of Black Carbon in the Climate System: A Scientific Assessment." *Journal of Geophysical Research: Atmosphere* 118: 5380–5552.

Buseck, P. R., K. Adachi, A. Gelencsér, E. Tompa, and M. Pósfai. 2014. "Ns-soot: A Material-Based Term for Strongly Light-Absorbing Carbonaceous Particles." *Aerosol Science and Technology* 48: 777–88.

Bush, B., G. Anno, R. McCoy, R. Gaj, and R. D. Small. 1991. "Fuel Loads in U.S. Cities." *Fire Technology* 27: 5–32.

Carrier, G. F. 1990. "Nuclear Winter, Current Understanding." *Proceedings of the American Philosophical Society* 134: 83–89.

Carrier, G. F., F. E. Fendell, and P. S. Feldman. 1984. "Big Fires." *Combustion Science and Technology* 107: 135–62.

Carrier, G. F., F. E. Fendell, and P. S. Feldman, "Firestorms." 1985. *Journal of Heat Transfer* 39: 19–27.

Chandler, C., P. Cheney, P. Thomas, L. Trabaud, and D. Williams. 1983. *Fire in Forestry, vol. 2: Forest Fire Management and Organization,* chapter 8 (New York: Wiley).

Chin, M., R. F. Kahn, and S. E. Schwartz, eds. 2009. *Atmospheric Aerosol Properties and Climate Impacts: Synthesis and Assessment Product 2.3,* report by the US Climate Change Science Program and the Subcommittee on Global Change Research. Washington, DC: NASA, http://downloads.globalchange.gov/sap/sap2-3/sap2-3-final-report-all.pdf.

Crutzen, P. J. 1984. "Darkness after Nuclear War." *AMBIO* 13: 52–54.

Crutzen, P. J., and J. W. Birks. 1982. "The Atmosphere after a Nuclear War: Twilight at Noon." *AMBIO* 11: 114–25.

Crutzen, P. J., I. E. Galbally, and C. Brühl. 1984. "Atmospheric Effects from Post-nuclear Fires." *Climatic Change* 6: 323–64.

Culver, C. G. 1978. "Characteristics of Fire Loads in Office Buildings." *Fire Technology* 14: 51–60.

de Laat, A. T. J., D. C. Stein Zweers, R. Boers, and O. N. E. Tuinder. 2012. "A Solar Escalator: Observational Evidence of the Self-Lifting of Smoke and Aerosols by Absorption of Solar Radiation in the February 2009 Australian Black Saturday Plume." *Journal of Geophysical Research* 117.

Dolan, P. J., ed. 1972. "Capabilities of Nuclear Weapons, Defense Nuclear Agency Effects Manual no. 1, parts 1 (Phenomenology) and 2 (Damage Criteria)." Defense Technical Information Center, http://www.dtic.mil/docs/citations/ADA955403 and http://www.dtic.mil/docs/citations/ADA955391.

Eden, L. 2006. *Whole World on Fire* (Ithaca, NY: Cornell University Press).

Glasstone, S., and P. J. Dolan. 1977. *The Effects of Nuclear Weapons.* 3rd ed. Washington, DC: US Department of Defense and Energy Research and Development Administration.

Jeanloz, R. 2012. "Long-Range Effects of Nuclear Disasters," in *The Nuclear Enterprise, High Consequence Accidents: How to Enhance Safety and Minimize Risks in Nuclear Weapons and Reactors*. Edited by G. P. Shultz and S. D. Drell. Stanford, CA: Hoover Press, 107–26.

Kerber, S. 2012. "Analysis of Changing Residential Fire Dynamics and Its Implications on Firefighter Operational Timeframes." *Fire Technology* 48: 865–91.

Malone, R. C., L. H. Auer, G. A. Glatzmaier, M. C. Wood, and O. B. Toon. 1986. "Nuclear Winter: Three-Dimensional Simulations Including Interactive Transport, Scavenging, and Solar Heating of Smoke." *Journal of Geophysical Research* 91: 1039–53.

Marshall, E. 1987. "Nuclear Winter Debate Heats Up." *Science* 235: 271–73.

Mills, M. J., O. B. Toon, R. P. Turco, D. E. Kinnison, and R. R. Garcia. 2008. "Massive Global Ozone Loss Predicted Following Regional Nuclear Conflict." *Proceedings of the National Academy of Sciences* 105: 5307–12.

Mills, M. M., O. B. Toon, J. Lee-Taylor, and A. Robock. 2014. "Multidecadal Global Cooling and Unprecedented Ozone Loss Following a Regional Nuclear Conflict." *Earth's Future* 2: 161–76.

National Fire Protection Association (NFPA). 2003. *Fire Protection Handbook, vol.2.* 19th ed. 12.93–112.

National Research Council (NRC). 1985. *The Effects on the Atmosphere of a Major Nuclear Exchange*. Washington, DC: National Academies Press, http://www.nap.edu/catalog/540/the-effects-on-the-atmosphere-of-a-major-nuclear-exchange.

National Research Council (NRC). 1986. *The Medical Implications of Nuclear War*. Washington, DC: National Academies Press, http://www.nap.edu/catalog/940/the-medical-implications-of-nuclear-war.

National Research Council (NRC). 2005. *Effects of Nuclear Earth-Penetrator and Other Weapons*. Washington, DC: National Academies Press, http://www.nap.edu/catalog/11282/effects-of-nuclear-earth-penetrator-and-other-weapons.

Office of Technology Assessment (OTA). 1979. *The Effects of Nuclear War*. Washington, DC: US Government Printing Office, http://ota.fas.org/reports/7906.pdf.

Oreskes, N., and E. M. Conway. 2011. *Merchants of Doubt: How a Handful of Scientists Obscured the Truth on Issues from Tobacco Smoke to Global Warming*. New York: Bloomsbury Press.

Özdogan, M., A. Robock, and C. J. Kucharik, 2013. "Impact of a Nuclear War in South Asia on Soybean and Maize Production in the Midwest United States." *Climate Change* 116: 373–87.

Pitts, W. M. 1991. "Wind Effects on Fires." *Progress in Energy and Combustion Sciences* 17: 83–134.

Pósfai, M., and P. R. Buseck. 2010. "Nature and Climate Effects of Individual Tropospheric Aerosol Particles." *Annual Review of Earth and Planetary Sciences* 38: 17–43.

Rehm, R. G., A. Hamins, H. R. Baum, K. B. McGrattan, and D. D. Evans. 2002. "Community-Scale Fire Spread." National Institute of Standards and Technology, http://fire.nist.gov/bfrlpubs/fire02/art019.html

Robock, A., L. Oman, and G. L. Stenchikov. 2007a. "Nuclear Winter Revisited with a Modern Climate Model and Current Nuclear Arsenals: Still Catastrophic Consequences." *Journal of Geophysical Research* 112.

Robock, A., L. Oman, G. L. Stenchikov, O. B. Toon, C. G. Bardeen, and R. P. Turco. 2007b. "Climatic Consequences of Regional Nuclear Conflicts." *Atmospheric Chemistry and Physics* 7: 2003–12.

Sagan, C., R. Turco, G. W. Rathjens, R. H. Siegel, S. L. Thompson, and S. H. Schneider. 1986. "The Nuclear Winter Debate." *Foreign Affairs* 65: 163–78.

Sakharov, A. 1968. "Progress, Coexistence and Intellectual Freedom." Sakharov Center, http://www.sakharov-center.ru/asfconf2011/english/articleseng/1.

Siddaway, J. M., and S. V. Petelina. 2011. "Transport and Evolution of the 2009 Australian Black Saturday Bushfire Smoke in the Lower Stratosphere Observed by OSIRIS on Odin." *Journal of Geophysical Research* 116.

Small, R. D. 1989. "Atmospheric Smoke Loading from a Nuclear Attack on the United States." *AMBIO* 18: 377–83.

Small, R. D., and B. W. Bush. 1985. "Smoke Production from Multiple Nuclear Explosions in Nonurban Areas." *Science* 229: 465–69.

Soden, B. J., R. T. Wettherald, G. L. Stenchikov, and A. Robock. 2002. "Global Cooling after the Eruption of Mount Pinatubo: A Test of Climate Feedback by Water Vapor." *Science* 296: 727–30.

Stenke, A., C. R. Hoyle, B. Luo, E. Rozanov, J. Gröbner, L. Maag, S. Brönnimann, and T. Peter. 2013. "Climate and Chemistry Effects of a Regional Scale Nuclear Conflict." *Atmospheric Chemistry and Physics* 13: 9713–29.

Thompson, S. L., V. V. Aleksandrov, G. L. Stenchikov, S. H. Schneider, C. Covey, and R. M. Chervin. 1984. "Global Climate Consequences of Nuclear War: Simulations with Three Dimensional Models." *AMBIO* 13: 236–43.

Toon, O. B., A. Robock, and R. P. Turco. 2008. "Environmental Consequences of Nuclear War." *Physics Today* 61: 37–42.

Toon, O. B., R. P. Turco, A. Robock, C. G. Bardeen, L. Oman, and G. L. Stenchikov. 2007. "Atmospheric Effects and Societal Consequences of Regional Scale Nuclear Conflicts and Acts of Individual Nuclear Terrorism." *Atmospheric Chemistry and Physics* 7: 1973–2002, and *Atmospheric Chemistry and Physics Discuss.* 6: S6992–S7001.

Trenberth, K. E., and A. Dai. 2007. "Effects of Mount Pinatubo Volcanic Eruption on the Hydrological Cycle as an Analog of Geoengineering." *Geophysics Research Letters* 34.

Turco, R. P., O. B. Toon, T. P. Ackerman, J. B. Pollack, and C. Sagan. 1983. "Nuclear Winter: Global Consequences of Multiple Nuclear Explosions." *Science* 222: 1283–292.

Turco, R. P., O. B. Toon, T. P. Ackerman, J. B. Pollack, and C. Sagan. 1990. "Climate and Smoke: An Appraisal of Nuclear Winter." *Science* 247: 166–76.

Turco, R. P., O. B. Toon, T. P. Ackerman, J. B. Pollack, and C. Sagan. 1991. "Nuclear Winter: Physics and Physical Mechanisms." *Annual Review of Earth and Planetary Sciences* 19: 383–422.

Utyuzhnikov, S. V. 2013. "Numerical and Laboratory Prediction of Smoke Lofting in the Atmosphere over Large Area Fires." *Applied Mathematical Modelling* 37: 876–87.

Xia, L., and A. Robock. 2013. "Impacts of a Nuclear War in South Asia on Rice Production in Mainland China." *Climate Change* 116: 357–72.

Decoding the Biosphere and the Infectious Disease Threat

Lucy Shapiro

We are in the midst of a revolution in the biosciences that has created technologies able to decode and manipulate the genetic information of all living entities on our planet. This revolution has resulted in unprecedented breakthroughs in medical therapies, diagnostics, and the design of novel sources of energy. Of particular importance is insight into the global ecosystem that faces perturbation due to climate change. Along with unquestioned value to biomedical science, these technologies have consequences that raise moral and ethical issues that resonate with the vision and cautions that Andrei Sakharov posited fifty years ago, but in a very different and unanticipated arena.

It was a mere sixty years ago that the instructions used by every living cell to direct the business of life were shown by James Watson and Francis Crick to reside in a DNA double helix. During the past twenty years, there has been an explosion in our ability to sequence the DNA, not only of humans, but of all life forms, including viruses, bacteria, fungi, and protozoa, many of which are included in the pathogen army with which we are engaged in an ongoing war to protect the health and continued maintenance of the human species. We can read the DNA sequence (universal instruction blueprint) of a virus in hours, and in a day or two obtain the far more complex sequence of a bacterial pathogen. This rapid identification of potential pathogens has presented new avenues of medical and forensic diagnostics. Critically, we now have the ability to engineer the genes encoded in DNA so that we change their sequence and thus their function—for example, changing the ability of viruses to infect specific hosts or generating viruses that are transmissible through the air. Further, we can recombine genes among different organisms, thereby creating, in essence, new life forms that carry out specific functions, such as the breakdown of cellulose to generate biofuels or the manipulation of DNA to create a highly lethal pathogen. A concern is the dual use of these tools on the one hand to identify viruses for vaccine production and pandemic control and on the other hand to promote their use as potential biological weapons.

Case Study

Every year, infection with an influenza virus kills five hundred thousand people globally and approximately fifty thousand people in the United States. This virus mutates easily, changing the proteins on the surface of the virus so that they are unique to a particular strain of virus. The major surface proteins on the flu virus to which we generate vaccines each year are called haemaglutinin (H) and neuraminidase (N). H binds to host cells to aid virus entry and N allows newly formed viruses to escape and infect other host cells. Periodically, we are faced with a global pandemic: the 1918 flu (H1N1) killed about fifty million people; the 1957 flu (H2N2) killed about two million people; the 1968 flu (H3N2) killed about one million people. The latest pandemic was in 2009, but was less severe to humans. The vectors for these viruses are generally birds and pigs. It is when these viruses become transmissible among humans that pandemics occur. We are currently faced with a global challenge: a new flu strain, H5N1, was first detected in 1997 in Hong Kong bird populations. It then spread throughout Southeast Asia followed by its appearance globally via migratory birds. The first transmission from birds to humans was detected in 2003. Since its appearance in humans, six hundred people have been infected, with an unprecedented kill rate of almost 60 percent. (The 1918 flu had a kill rate of only 2 percent, but it was wildly infectious.) As of now, this virus is not transmissible (airborne) among humans, but it is continually mutating and evolving so it presents a clear danger as a potential transmissible pandemic strain.

To stay ahead of this evolving potential pandemic strain of flu, scientists are asking several questions: Is there an identifiable genetic signature for a pandemic H5N1 flu that can be used for surveillance? Is there a genetic signature that identifies a strain of flu with a high kill rate? If this pandemic strain evolved, would it be sensitive to existing H5N1 non-pandemic vaccines and would it still be sensitive to existing drugs? The execution of laboratory experiments to address these questions has led to a collision of knowledge-driven science and ethical considerations. In effect, does the anticipated good outweigh the predictable bad? Recently, these issues were brought into stark reality when two laboratories, one in Wisconsin and the other in the Netherlands, carried out experiments to genetically engineer and evolve a strain of H5N1 flu that is transmissible on respiratory droplets among ferrets, the model organism most like the human in its response to infection by flu. As in humans, the flu virus gains entry into its ferret host by attaching to cells in the airways, and ferrets sneeze when infected. These laboratories succeeded in generating a pathogenic strain of the H5N1 flu virus that is airborne and transmissible among ferrets. Sequence analysis revealed that it took five mutations in two genes of the virus to make it transmissible. These studies provided incremental information about the mechanisms used for transmissibility. To date, the mutated virus appears to be vulnerable to existing vaccines and flu drugs and there is no evidence that these mutant strains can, in fact, infect humans. However, alarms were triggered when the two labs first attempted to publish their work in 2011. The National Science Advisory Board for Biosecurity (NSABB), an independent federal advisory committee, called a halt to the publication of these papers out of concern for biosecurity. This act generated international concern, discussion, and disagreement among scientists, akin to the debate held at the Asilomar Conference led by Paul Berg in the 1970s when recombinant DNA technology first was published. In both cases, scientists worried that bioterrorists might use genetically altered strains or that the virulent pathogens might accidentally escape from labs with even the highest biosafety secure protocols. As a result of these discussions, the scientific community called for moratoria on continued experiments until oversight committees could be established. Ultimately, the NSABB agreed that the research is important for public health and should be published in its entirety. In March 2012, the US government announced the establishment of the US Government Policy for Oversight of Life Sciences Dual Use Research of Concern with a mandate to oversee federal funding of dual use research, to assess the risks and benefits, and to develop risk mitigation protocols. With this in place, work on flu viruses resumed in 2013.

The Situation Today

The most recent federal response to research on dual use pathogens (October 2014) has called for a one-year "pause" to develop a new policy. This response by the federal government is fueled by reports of mishandled samples at the Centers for Disease Control and Prevention and by continued concerns about research on flu (the 1918 flu virus has recently been reconstructed in the lab) and the SARS (severe acute respiratory syndrome) and MERS (Middle East respiratory syndrome) viruses with enhanced transmissibility via the respiratory route. This mandated pause was developed by the Office of Science and Technology Policy and the Department of Health and Human Services. Multiple agencies, including the National Academy of Sciences, are poised to review the recommendations generated during this one-year pause to develop risk/benefit assessments.

We are at a critical junction between science and government policy. At issue are the responsibility of individual scientists to the public interest and the responsibility of the public, and particularly policymakers, to understand and respond appropriately to the science in question. We must deal in facts, not political expediency, and to do so we need a more scientifically literate public. We are faced with two critical questions: What is the proper and ultimately effective role of government in regulating science? Should science, in fact, be regulated? Innovation in scientific research remains the bedrock of US prominence in the international scientific and technology arena and of our unparalleled economic success. We impede discovery and innovation at our peril. Currently, the funding and regulation of science are subject to competing stakeholders who see the relevance of scientific research within the context of their own concerns: businesses seeking profits, universities seeking federal grant support, patients seeking cures, and politicians seeking support for their agendas.

I posit that ethical policy positions related to global health cannot help but be rooted in scientific insight that is viewed through the lens of the infectious disease threat, globalization and its consequences, and environmental challenges such as climate change.

Diagnosis, Reinvented for the Individual

Elizabeth Holmes

In 1986, Andrei Sakharov was freed after years of living in exile and under house arrest for speaking up for the people in his country who were oppressed, demanding that his country be for peace and stop testing the nuclear weapons he helped design, and championing the belief that fundamental human rights exist for all. His courage to stand up for his principles never wavered—not when he had a guard outside his door, a jamming station preventing foreign radio signals, and no access to a telephone—and that resolve grew even stronger when he stood as a liberated man. Some of his first words in freedom were to call for the release of all "prisoners of conscience." He declared: "I will never abandon the fight for human freedom. Peace depends on the freedom of each and every man." Sakharov's call for human rights and individual freedom still lives on for those everywhere who struggle for justice, for scientists who live in repressive regimes, and for individuals like me who share in his commitment to and belief in the basic human rights defined in the United Nations' Universal Declaration of Human Rights.

One particular belief underlying that declaration is at the core of my life's work: everyone has the right to protect his or her own health and the well-being of those he or she loves. Yet in the United States today, that right is often denied. We see that lack of justice when health care bills contribute to most bankruptcies[1] and in the suffering of individuals when they find out too late in the disease-progression process that they are sick.

I had a loved one suffer, and lose his life, because he was diagnosed too late. I grew up spending summers and holidays with my uncle. I remember his love of crossword puzzles and trying to teach us to play football. I remember how much he loved the beach. I remember how much I loved him. One day, he was diagnosed with skin cancer that suddenly turned to brain cancer and spread to his bones. He did not live to see his son grow up, and I never got to say goodbye.

Medical "diagnosis" is defined as the determination of the presence of disease from its signs and symptoms. Yet for millions of people just like my uncle, disease begins much earlier than when the mole on the skin changes color, the foot starts to throb in pain, or shortness of breath makes playing with a niece or a nephew too difficult. That is why individuals must be given the right to access the information they need when it matters most: when they still have the opportunity to change their lives and before a disease latches on with its fatal grip.

Technology is rapidly transforming health care, and we need to use new, life-saving technology to save more lives. Laboratory information is so important that it drives 70 to 80 percent of clinical decisions.[2] Yet there are tremendous impediments to individual access to that critical, life-saving data. Until recently, people in many states could not get copies of their own lab results for tests ordered for them by their physicians, even if they paid for it.[3] There are other impediments to giving individuals access to information about their health, including laws across the country that prohibit one's ability to order a lab test without a physician's order. I can buy a deadly exotic animal like a venomous viper, a military truck, or an armored vehicle—I can buy a tank which, a quick search of the Internet provides, "is generally available for any budget or situation"—but, in many parts of the United States, I still cannot order a blood-based pregnancy test or an allergy test because that could be dangerous. God forbid I stop eating peanuts!

In order to engage an individual in changing health care outcomes, she must be put in the driver's seat of her own care, and that begins with access to the information to do so. A woman trying to conceive a child should be able to order a fertility test on her own. With 110 million cases of sexually transmitted infections in the United States, all of which are treatable, someone worried about risk should be able to order an STI test.[4] When individuals have access to information about their bodies, they can engage in their own health care and begin to change outcomes. Type 2 diabetes alone, which drives 20 percent of our health care costs,[5] can be reversed through changes in lifestyle, such as diet and exercise. Yet today, there are 80 million Americans who are pre-diabetic, and 90 percent of them do not even know it.[6] Another 15 percent of our health care costs are associated with whether an individual makes the choice to be compliant with prescriptions written by physicians.[7]

Yet, there are barriers that continue to deny people their right to access the health information they need. In addition to legal barriers in some states, our research shows that as many as 60 percent of people do not fulfill a physician-ordered lab test—tests that are ordered once someone is already symptomatic for a given condition. A key reason so many do not comply is accessibility. They cannot afford the test; even for those who are insured, the deductibles can amount to a few hundred dollars out of pocket. Plus, locations and hours for lab testing can make tests inaccessible for those who do not have the means to take time away from work. Another reason is needles; fear of needles is a basic human fear that affects at least one in ten people.[8] All the advances in science and technology will have limitations if we do not remove the obstacles to people using them. Sakharov taught us that extraordinary changes must not only be purposeful and meaningful, but they must be in concert with strengthening human rights and benefiting all of mankind.

My life's work in building Theranos is to redefine the paradigm of diagnosis away from one in which people have to present with symptoms in order to get access to information about their bodies to one in which all people, no matter how much money they have or where they live, have access to health information in time to prevent disease and other illness.

Over the last eleven years, Theranos has proven that it is possible to advance science and technology through a patient-centered business model. We look at lab testing from the patients' point of view. They want low-cost, easily accessible, pain-free access to their health information. We have made it possible to run any laboratory test for 50 to 90 percent off of Medicare reimbursement rates. We have made it possible to run comprehensive laboratory tests from a tiny sample—a few drops of blood—that can be taken from a painless prick of the finger. We have made it possible to eliminate the tubes and tubes of blood that traditionally have to be drawn from an arm, and have replaced it with the Nanotainer. We have made it possible for useful information to be accessible at the time and place that matters—near where people live and where they see their physicians. And we have made it possible for information to be accessible by creating a decentralized infrastructure overseen by a centralized lab. We have done those things because we envision a different world.

I see a world in which every person knows how much a test is going to cost them before they get that test done—every time. I remember listening to a woman who came to one of our wellness centers to get tested. She talked about a conversation with her physician in which she raised her concerns about the risk of hereditary diseases that had afflicted her family, and she asked to get a series of tests done. The physician said to her, "Well, insurance isn't going to cover this. Do you still want to do it?" And she said, "Yes. How much does it cost?" Her physician did not know. She determined that it was likely to cost her a few thousand dollars to get these tests done—tests for conditions for which she was not yet symptomatic—and she could not afford that. People will go bankrupt if they have to spend thousands of dollars out of pocket in order to get the tests they need to begin to understand their risks of a condition before they develop it. I'll always remember the face of a pregnant woman who showed up at one of our locations after she had been turned away from the other labs because she could not afford the test she needed. She was so scared that she was going to be turned away by us, too. When she saw the cost of the tests would be a little more than the cost of a meal, the gratitude on her face struck my heart. No person should have to go through that fear.

I see a world in which no one has to go through the pain of traditional phlebotomy. I remember reading an e-mail from the father of a little girl. He talked about taking her to the hospital and watching as they stuck her soft tissue again and again in the search for what he called "the tiny, invisible vein." I have met elderly people with veins collapsed due to age who had to get blood drawn through the hand, which caused so much pain. And I have spoken to cancer patients who say that they can take the treatments, the radiation, and the visits to the hospital—but the fear, bruising, and transfusions associated with all the endless blood draws break them, and those who love and care for them, down.

I see a world in which people get access to laboratory information late at night, on a weekend, early in the morning, and in rural areas. By establishing decentralized and distributed testing frameworks, we see a world in which care begins to become possible in underserved and developing economies—places where people still read Sakharov's work, not for insights into the past, but for the strength and guidance on how to shape their future in a way that is just and strengthens individuals' rights.

Sakharov advised that, in an age of great transformation, science and the conscience must be connected. He said at the close of his Nobel Lecture, "We must make good the demands of reason and create a life worthy of ourselves and of the goals we only dimly perceive." We have a right to engage with information about ourselves, about our bodies. Technological innovations make it possible to know about health issues before symptoms arise, and scientific advances give us options for what to do with that information. By building on Sakharov's commitment to fighting for human rights, including the right to health care etched in the United Nation's declaration, we can build a world in which all people have access to the health information they need; a world in which no one has to say, "If only I'd known sooner"; a world in which no one has to say goodbye too soon. That is a world I will continue to fight for until it is more than one we dimly perceive, but is brightly lit, and benefits the health and rights of every individual.

Notes

1. David U. Himmelstein, Deborah Thorne, Elizabeth Warren, and Steffie Woolhandler, "Medical Bankruptcy in the United States, 2007: Results of a National Study," *American Journal of Medicine* 122, no. 8 (August 2009): 741–46.

2. "Report of the Review of NHS Pathology Services in England: An Independent Review for the Department of Health," August 2006, 5.

3. US Department of Health and Human Services, "HHS Strengthens Patients' Right to Access Lab Test Reports," news release, February 3, 2014, http://www.hhs.gov/news/press/2014pres/02/20140203a .html.

4. Centers for Disease Control, "Incidence, Prevalence, and Cost of Sexually Transmitted Infections in the United States," February 2013, http://www.cdc.gov/std/stats/sti-estimates-fact-sheet-feb-2013.pdf.

5. Jane E. Brody, "Averting Diabetes before It Takes Hold," *Personal Health* (blog), *New York Times,* September 8, 2014, http://well.blogs .nytimes.com/2014/09/08/prediabetes-blood-sugar/?_r=0.

6. Ibid.

7. George Hofmann, "Medication Compliance: Why Don't We Take Our Meds?" *Psych Central,* May 2, 2013, http://psychcentral.com /blog/archives/2013/05/02/medication-compliance-why-dont-we -take-our-meds/.

8. James G. Hamilton, "Needle Phobia: A Neglected Diagnosis," *Journal of Family Practice* 41, no. 2 (August 1995): 169–75.

The Sakharov Conditions, Disruptive Technologies, and Human Rights

Christopher Stubbs

This paper explores the interplay between human rights, technology, and disruptive political change. Ever-increasing access to trusted information and rapid mass communication mechanisms, through smartphones and similar technologies, provide catalysts that can drive rapid political changes.

The context for this discussion is set by a remarkably prescient quote from a piece written in 1974 by Andrei Sakharov that bears directly on the topics explored below.[1] Bear in mind that this was written long before the advent of the personal computer, the Internet, or cell phones.

> I foresee a universal information system (UIS), which will give everyone access at any given moment to the contents of any book that has ever been published or any magazine or any fact. The

I am most grateful for the Annenberg Fellowship that provides my affiliation with the Hoover Institution, and which gives me the privilege of engaging in vibrant intellectual interactions with George Shultz, Sidney Drell, and other participants in its workshops and meetings. Enrique Oti drew the White House document on cyberspace to my attention during the workshop, for which I am most grateful. Thanks also to Carrington Gregory for insightful and helpful comments on this manuscript.

UIS will have individual miniature-computer terminals, central control points for the flood of information, and communication channels incorporating thousands of artificial communications from satellites, cables, and laser lines. Even the partial realization of the UIS will profoundly affect every person, his leisure activities, and his intellectual and artistic development. Unlike television . . . the UIS will give each person maximum freedom of choice and will require individual activity. But the true historic role of the UIS will be to break down the barriers to the exchange of information among countries and people.

Many, but not all, aspects of Sakharov's vision of the future have come to pass. Recent events demonstrate how access to disruptive technologies and communication networks can catalyze changes that can drive political systems out of equilibrium. The challenge, again illustrated by recent events, is to arrive at a new stable political equilibrium that respects individual liberties and human rights.

In his work as a scientist, Sakharov recognized the importance of out-of-equilibrium conditions in the early universe. The next section takes this concept into the human arena by considering the role of disruptive technologies in driving social and governmental systems out of equilibrium. Case studies are provided by recent events in both North Africa and Hong Kong. Access to evolving technologies and unfettered global information exchange are increasingly seen as fundamental civil liberties. Consequently, emerging technologies are playing a crucial role in the ever-evolving scope of what we consider basic human rights.

Disruptive Technology and Socio-Political Equilibrium

There is an extensive social science literature that considers the application of the concepts of equilibrium[2] and "punctuated equilibrium"[3] in the context of governmental and social systems. The basic idea is illustrated in figure 7.1. This is a notional figure where the vertical axis is some measure of instability, such as nondemocratic governmental changes per decade. Situations that are socially and politically stable are indicated by valleys and unstable circumstances by peaks.

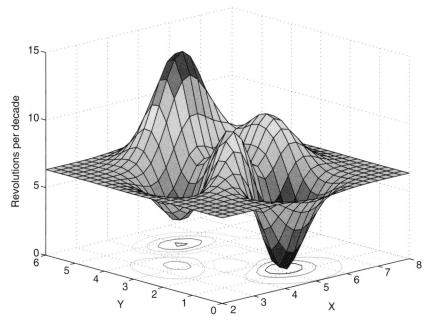

Figure 7.1. A notional social equilibrium surface. This notional diagram illustrates the concept of social and governmental equilibrium. The vertical axis might be the rate of revolutionary governmental change, per decade, while X might represent the annual growth percentage in GDP and Y the number of political parties.

In this formulation, social and governmental systems can settle into one of a number of long-term-stable configurations, but can be driven out of equilibrium if disrupted, or if one or more of the driving factors (economic, cultural, or political) change over time. Looking at the diversity of governments around the world, one can surmise that there are numerous equilibrium systems of governance, including dictatorships, monarchies, one-party governments, and a spectrum of implementations of democracy.

Western democracies aspire to maintain an equilibrium situation in which their citizens are economically secure, where individual rights are protected by the state, and where freedom of expression and freedom of religion are combined with an orderly and democratic changeover in representational government. But this circumstance currently eludes many countries, some of which are experiencing extended periods out of equilibrium.

In the context of figure 7.1, one should envision each society as a ball that rolls around on the two-dimensional surface, with some amount of friction. Stable equilibrium points are the bottoms of the valleys, and it takes a large perturbation to shift societies out of those stability points. Unstable equilibria reside at the peaks, where even a small nudge can induce a large shift in social conditions.

Figure 7.1 is meant to convey the notion of societies "settling into" stable equilibrium configurations that are shown as the upward-concave regions. But a sufficiently large disruption can push the system into an unstable situation, which will eventually result in a new equilibrium condition. This section will consider the role of personal technology access in driving major social and governmental change. We will use two recent examples: the "Arab Spring" uprisings and the ongoing (at this writing) pro-democracy demonstrations in Hong Kong.

Various authors have explored the role that technology, connectivity, and social media played in North Africa during the 2010–2012 Arab Spring political upheavals.[4] One school of thought holds that the speed at which public expressions of dissent and (in the cases of Tunisia, Egypt, Libya, and Yemen) regime change occurred is directly attributable to the "political feedback" due to interactions occurring over social media. Another point of view holds that the role of social media has been exaggerated, and that long-standing internal tensions simply boiled over in rapid succession.[5]

There is little doubt, however, of how technology and connectivity were seen by the governments that were under pressure. In both Egypt and Libya, the governments that were clinging to power took rather clumsy steps to suppress their citizens' access to Internet communications.[6] So these governments certainly perceived a threat arising from social media and from information transfer over the Internet. Their response was a heavy-handed attempt to cut off domestic Internet connectivity. But since the Internet was designed to be robust, with resilience against dropouts in one or more links, during the Arab Spring the citizens established and exploited connection pathways that sidestepped the government-controlled (and government-suppressed) information links.

A second example of modern technology playing a central role in public dissent is the 2014 pro-democracy movement in Hong Kong. Images of the crowds showed thousands of people waving their phones in the air, which is particularly apt given the rapidly evolving technological arms race between the demonstrators and their government. Gatherings were initially organized using social media tools.[7] The next step in the technical confrontation was an attempt (attributed by many to the Chinese government) to entice people to download a virus-like application onto their smartphones that provided access to stored personal data on the phone.[8] The protesters then in turn adapted by shifting to a direct phone-to-phone communication scheme (using the Bluetooth protocol) that entirely circumvented the government-controlled cell phone and Internet systems, thereby sidestepping the "Great Firewall of China."

In both the Arab Spring and Hong Kong examples, the governmental apparatus perceived the combination of dissent and technology to be sufficiently threatening that steps were taken to suppress, disrupt, or manipulate internal communications and/or information exchange with the outside world. This response alone is evidence for the important role of technology and instantaneous communications in contemporary political struggles, in which people attempt to assert their rights and realize their aspirations.

There are also equilibrium (or perhaps meta-stable equilibrium?) nation-states that routinely limit their citizens' access to information. A particularly dynamic situation at present is the Islamic Republic of Iran, which recently established a Supreme Council for Cyberspace, while simultaneously slightly relaxing the restrictions placed on social media access.[9] In the framework of figure 7.1, this is an attempt by the government to retain equilibrium (and power) by addressing the changing expectations among its populace with adjustments in its technology policy. China also exerts tight control over information access by and between its citizens. Web sites are blacklisted by the tens of thousands,[10] and as many as 16 percent of the postings on social media sites are deleted by censors.[11]

The moves and counter-moves in cyberspace taken by governments and their citizens create a dynamic situation. The marketplace penetration of smartphones is a critical factor that determines their political impact. There is a steady increase in individual access to technology; according to one market analysis, by 2017 we can expect 69 percent of the world's population to own a mobile phone, and at that point half of these devices are expected to be smartphones with web connectivity and the ability to run applications and exchange text messages and photographs.[12] Access to this technology is rapidly increasing, along with the role it plays in our lives. The impact of this technology in disruptive political situations can only increase, until we reach the saturation point where phone-mediated information can rapidly reach the majority of people, either directly or through people around them who have phones.

Is Technology Access a Basic Human Right?

The consensus view of the scope of human rights and individual liberty evolves. Slavery is now unthinkable in developed nations, and same-sex marriage is gaining increasing acceptance across the United States. Technology has the ability to affect virtually all aspects of our lives; parenting, education, commerce and finance, and entertainment are components of modern life that are undergoing fundamental changes driven by evolving technology. It is therefore no surprise that the nexus between technology, individual freedom of expression, and human rights is also changing.

Article 19 of the United Nations' Universal Declaration of Human Rights asserts:

> Everyone has the right to freedom of opinion and expression; this right includes freedom to hold opinions without interference and to seek, receive and impart information and ideas through any media and regardless of frontiers.[13]

Should this be interpreted as a guarantee of access to any Internet site by any individual? Does technology access constitute a human right, or simply a framework for freedom of expression? These questions are unresolved. This is an area of current public discourse, with one faction arguing in favor of a broad interpretation of Article 19. Others maintain that technology-mediated information access can *empower* human rights but is not such a right unto itself.

We are not yet, and may never be, at the point where individual technology access is a *universally* recognized human right. But there seems no doubt that we are witnessing a rapid evolution in the relationships between individuals, their governments, and personal-scale information technology. Individual access to information technology is increasing rapidly. This is driven by choices made by people who evidently highly value smartphone-mediated access to information, to banking services, and to one another.[14] The role of social media in disruptive political events has demonstrably increased even in the short time between the Arab Spring uprisings of a few years ago and today's demonstrations in Hong Kong.

The current US stance on cyber-access as a human right is described in the 2011 White House document on cyberspace strategy.[15] The document identifies "the ability to seek, receive and impart information and ideas through any medium and regardless of frontiers" as a fundamental freedom, and declares that the US policy is to protect, promote, and facilitate this human right.

The Sakharov Conditions, and Equilibrium in the Early Universe

As we gather to honor Andrei Sakharov's legacy in human rights and in arms control, we should also pause to recognize his scientific accomplishments. This piece therefore closes with a brief summary of Sakharov's scientific insight into why the universe has the properties we observe.

Cosmologists attempt to understand the contents and structure of the universe within a framework of fundamental physics. One basic goal of cosmology is to understand the ingredients of the cosmos. All of our observations are consistent with the idea that the universe started in a dense hot state, from which it expanded and cooled. As the universe cooled, it cascaded through the energy domains we associate with particle physics, to nuclear physics, to atomic physics, to astrophysics. One of the triumphs of the big bang model is the precise agreement between nuclear physics calculations and the observations of the relative abundances of lightweight primordial elements (hydrogen, helium, and lithium).

To place Sakharov's cosmology work in context, we need to quickly review the concept of antimatter. Every elementary particle in nature has a twin anti-particle. We can routinely create matched pairs of protons and anti-protons, electrons and antielectrons, neutrons and anti-neutrons in accelerators like the one here at Stanford's SLAC National Accelerator Laboratory. These anti-particles have electrical charges that are the opposite of their regular-matter partners, but their masses are identical. Anti-protons carry an electrical charge that is equal and opposite to the positive charge carried by protons, for example.

But in the freezing-out of "substance" from the initially superheated primordial plasma, something strange must have happened. The simplest scenario would predict equal amounts of matter and antimatter, produced in matching pairs. But when we look out at the Milky Way galaxy and beyond, we see no evidence for any primordial antimatter at all—anywhere. The simplest scenario is therefore clearly wrong.

The overwhelming cosmic preponderance of matter over antimatter is a real mystery. Given the apparent intrinsic symmetry between matter and antimatter, what could prompt the preference for one over the other? Andrei Sakharov took up this intellectual challenge. In 1967 he published a paper that set forth three conditions (known throughout the cosmology community as the "Sakharov conditions") that, if satisfied, would lead to a preference for matter over antimatter in the evolution of the universe.[16]

One might think that simply breaking the matter-antimatter symmetry in some fundamental process would suffice, but Sakharov taught us that it takes more than that.

The Sakharov conditions for producing an excess of matter over antimatter are:[17]

1. There must exist an interaction or process that somehow intrinsically favors protons over anti-protons.

2. Two fundamental symmetries that physicists once thought sacrosanct must be invalid.[18]

3. There must be an episode during which these processes are occurring out of thermal equilibrium.

These Sakharov conditions for producing a cosmic matter-antimatter asymmetry are a cornerstone of modern cosmology. His 1967 paper has received over one thousand citations to date, and it continues to frame our thinking about how the big bang could have cooked up the ingredients of our universe. This lasting scientific legacy is an enduring testament to Sakharov's scientific intellect and insight, in addition to his well-deserved status as a champion of human rights and democratic values.

Notes

1. Andrei Sakharov, "Tomorrow: The View from Red Square," *Saturday Review*, August 24, 1974.

2. See, for example, Thomas J. Fararo, "General Social Equilibrium: Toward Theoretical Synthesis," *Sociological Theory* 11, no. 3 (1993): 291.

3. See, for example, Albert Somit and Steven Peterson, *The Dynamics of Evolution: The Punctuated Equilibrium Debate in the Natural and Social Sciences* (Ithaca, NY: Cornell University Press, 1992).

4. Philip N. Howard, Aiden Duffy, Deen Freelon, Muzammil Hussain, Will Mari, and Marwa Mazaid, "Opening Closed Regimes: What Was the Role of Social Media During the Arab Spring?" Project on Information Technology & Political Islam, University of Washington–Seattle, http://pitpi.org/wp-content/uploads/2013/02/2011_Howard-Duffy-Freelon-Hussain-Mari-Mazaid_pITPI.pdf; and Lord Guy Black, "The Arab Spring and the Impact of Social Media," Albany Association, http://www.albanyassociates.com/notebook/2012/03/the-arab-spring-and-the-impact-of-social-media/.

5. Anita Singh, "Ways with Words: Role of Twitter and Facebook in Arab Spring Uprising 'Overstated', Says Hisham Matar," *The Telegraph*, July 11, 2011, http://www.telegraph.co.uk/culture/books/ways-with-words/8629294/Ways-With-Words-role-of-Twitter-and-Facebook-in-Arab-Spring-uprising-overstated-says-Hisham-Matar.html.

6. Alberto Dainotti, Claudio Squarcella, Emile Aben, Kimberly C. Claffy, Marco Chiesa, Michele Russo, and Antonio Pescapé, "Analysis of Country-wide Internet Outages Caused by Censorship," Center for Applied Internet Data Analysis, http://www.caida.org/publications/papers/2011/outages_censorship/outages_censorship.pdf.

7. Emily Parker, "Social Media and the Hong Kong Protests," *The New Yorker* (online), October 1, 2014, http://www.newyorker.com /tech/elements/social-media-hong-kong-protests.

8. Paul Mozur, "Protesters in Hong Kong Are Targets of Scrutiny through Their Phones," *New York Times*, October 1, 2014, http://www .nytimes.com/2014/10/02/business/protesters-are-targets-of-scrutiny -through-their-phones.html?_r=0.

9. Thomas Erdbrink, "Iranians Gain Access to Facebook and Twitter," *New York Times*, September 16, 2013, http://www.nytimes.com/2013 /09/17/world/middleeast/iran-facebook-twitter-access.html?_r=0.

10. Jonathan Zittrain and Benjamin Edelman, "Empirical Analysis of Internet Filtering in China," Berkman Society, http://cyber.law.harvard .edu/filtering/china/.

11. David Bamman, Brendan O'Connor, and Noah A. Smith, "Censorship and Deletion Practices in Chinese Social Media," *First Monday* 17, no. 3 (March 5, 2012), http://journals.uic.edu/ojs/index.php/fm /article/view/3943/3169.

12. "Smartphone Users Worldwide Will Total 1.75 Billion in 2014," *eMarketer*, January 16, 2014, http://www.emarketer.com/Article /Smartphone-Users-Worldwide-Will-Total-175-Billion-2014/1010536.

13. United Nations, Universal Declaration of Human Rights, http:// www.un.org/en/documents/udhr/index.shtml.

14. Frank Langfitt, "Mobile Money Revolution Aids Kenya's Poor, Economy," *All Things Considered*, National Public Radio, January 5, 2011, http://www.npr.org/2011/01/05/132679772/mobile-money -revolution-aids-kenyas-poor-economy.

15. White House, "International Strategy for Cyberspace: Prosperity, Security, and Openness in a Networked World," http://www.whitehouse .gov/sites/default/files/rss_viewer/international_strategy_for_cyberspace .pdf.

16. Andrei Sakharov, "Violation of CP Invariance, C Asymmetry, and Baryon Asymmetry of the Universe," *Journal of Experimental and Theoretical Physics, Lett.*, 5 (1967).

17. I have taken the liberty of attempting a phrasing that favors clarity for nonspecialists over technical physics accuracy.

18. These are charge conjugation, C, which flips the sign of all quantum numbers such as electrical charge and baryon number, and the product CP where P is parity reversal, essentially a spatial reflection. For many years these were taken for granted as valid symmetries of nature, but they are not.

New Dilemmas in Ethics, Technology, and War: Sakharov's Principles in Today's World

James O. Ellis Jr.

In June 2014, the American Academy of Arts and Sciences began a study intended to review and rethink the elements of "just war" doctrine. In a letter to the members of the steering committee for the study, which he chairs, Scott Sagan began: "Several technology innovations and political developments are changing the nature of warfare today, in ways that pose complex challenges to traditional conceptions of just war doctrine. New technologies—including the use of drones, precision-guided weapons, and non-lethal munitions—have led both to optimism about the possibility of reducing collateral damage in war and to concerns about whether some states find it too easy to use force today. The growth of terrorism by non-state actors, the spread of weapons of mass destruction, and changing doctrines about the responsibility to protect civilians pose new questions about the appropriate legal rules and ethical norms governing decisions to use military force. Professional military lawyers play an increasingly important role in reviewing targeting policies and rules of engagement, at least in the United States, to ensure that military plans and operations are compliant with the laws of armed conflict. War crimes tribunals have grown in use, but raise new questions about whether

Andrei Sakharov, Stanford University, 1989. Photo by Harvey Lynch.

they encourage ruthless leaders to fight to the finish rather than accept resignation and exile. New knowledge about post-conflict medical system failures raises questions about both *jus post bellum* [justice after war] best practices and whether political leaders systematically underestimate the costs of going to war before they make decisions about military interventions."

The complexity to which Sagan alludes—the intertwining of technology, policy, politics, and law with the human, societal, and religious norms within which the spectrum of warfare may or may not occur—requires either careful parsing into its constituent elements or the application of broadly applicable principles. The former can fail to address the interrelationships that are so critical to understanding; the latter risks simplistic or superficial standards of little use to those charged with the responsibilities for policy, strategic, or tactical judgments, whether in the halls of power or in the chaos of combat. Ultimately, ethical leaders must instill or impose reason over impulse.

The author attempts to approach that divide, not by defining specific solutions but by selecting a number of important issues—some from Sagan's letter, others not—and considering these challenges from the perspective of principles articulated by Andrei Sakharov, the physicist who made a personal journey from Russian patriot, honored three times as a Hero of Socialist Labor, to citizen of the world and powerful advocate for both nuclear disarmament and, ultimately, global human rights, an effort for which he was awarded the Nobel Peace Prize. Sakharov's biographers describe him with a quote from an iconic Russian author, in "the involuntary cry which had once escaped from Pushkin's chest: 'Why the devil was I born in Russia with a mind and a heart?'"[1]

Born with a mind and a heart into a tumultuous Russia still reeling from war and revolution, "Andrei Sakharov's life virtually coincided with the Soviet era. The year he was born, 1921, the new regime became definitively established, and the first non-Soviet elections . . . were held in 1989—the year he died."[2] His life saw dramatic changes in his country, its policies and actions, and his perception of them. He saw the dangers of the technology he birthed—the hydrogen bomb—but also understood that, beyond the technology, it was the national policies that, shadowed and emboldened by that technology, increasingly threatened both the global order and individual rights. As his biographers note: "According to Sakharov, the danger of thermonuclear war was the *result* [emphasis added] of the military-technical standoff between the superpowers and the equilibrium of fear. But the real strategic problem was the standoff itself, fraught with global suicide. He found the solution in an area seemingly distant from nuclear missiles—in the observance of human rights."[3]

A basic tenet of complex military planning, with all its sources, references, guidance, and directives—often duplicative, sometimes divergent and conflicting—is to always begin with a clear understanding of what it is you are trying to accomplish. In military message terms, when all else fails, go back and read "Ref. A," the initial directive. It might be instructional to begin that way here and, using the framework of Sakharov's experience, examine carefully the title of this chapter and the AAAS study: "New Dilemmas in Ethics, Technology, and War."

The first word is *New*, implying that the challenges have not been seen before. We would argue that, in the realm of military experience, genuinely new challenges are rare; more common are old challenges faced in a new context. Indeed, the fact that we can see compelling relevance in the life and lessons of a man who died a quarter of a century ago argues that the changing and challenging character of emerging issues does not mean the absence of enduring issues. Technological advances are not new on the battlefield. History reminds us that—whether it was English longbows, repeating rifles, the machine guns, airplanes, and tanks of the Great War, radar and atomic weapons in the next, or precision guidance and sophisticated intelligence collection today—the basic goals of seeing the enemy first and shooting faster, farther, or more accurately remain truisms. The complexities of insurgencies—distinguishing friend or noncombatant from foe, deciding the difference between military supplies and village food stocks, and fighting in an urban environment with the foe "swimming in the sea of the people"[4]— are not new. Nor is the fact that the isolated and antiseptic battle for which the technology is often designed is rarely the reality and that, in an overmatched conflict, a clever and adaptive adversary bases his potential for success on denying you the technological advantages you bring to the fight.

The second word in the title of this work is *Dilemmas*. One definition of the term is "a usually undesirable or difficult choice, where the level of undesirability or degree of difficulty is in the eye and mind of the beholder, defined by societal, organizational, or personal norms." There is no doubt that such dilemmas exist but we need to be careful not to imply that they are universal; our dilemmas are not necessarily viewed as such by current or potential adversaries who may, in contrast, view our decision-making angst as unfathomable and weak and see it as their advantage, politically, societally, or militarily. Today's leaders, civilian and military, must deal with the asymmetry in conflicts where, in a sense, our ethical and moral code is a complicating factor or a weapon to be used against us when civilians are mixed into the battlefield, either accidentally or intentionally. This dilemma is even more stark in our current age when we find ourselves battling an enemy who has intentionally chosen to fight from among innocent noncombatants while at the same time expanding apocalyptically the definition of legitimate targets and continuing the boastful showcasing of ritual executions.

Discussions of ethical behavior often default to an appropriate question of standards. Any discussion of ethics on a cross-cultural, much less global, scale must accept that an agreed and shared framework is difficult to achieve even in the face of horrific actions or equally horrific consequences of inaction. Sakharov clearly believed in a universal human standard that may be increasingly difficult to achieve in a multiethnic, multipolar world: "I am convinced that the ideology of defending human rights is the only basis that can unite people independent of their nationality, politics, religion and social status."[5]

One dilemma confronting democratic societies is the advent of the all-volunteer force. The increasing use of complex technology and the demands of "professionalizing" a military with those who have the motivation and skills to serve have made conscription impractical, but it has also eliminated, at least in the United States, the concept of universal service. To the fundamental question of whether these forces fairly mirror the society that they serve has been added the speculation that national leadership may be more likely to employ a military to which it is less connected societally. Critics certainly overreach when they say we risk "outsourcing" our wars, but the implications of the military service and combat burden being borne by a smaller segment of society have yet to be fully analyzed.

A second dilemma facing civilian and military leaders is related to the "dichotomy of deterrence" that underpins classic nuclear strategy. The historic challenge that still confronts those who oversee or operate the nation's nuclear weapons complex, from the laboratories to the operators, is the fact that in order to deter an adversary and ensure that nuclear weapons will never be used there has to be created in the mind of an adversary the belief that, under the most extreme provocation, they would actually be used and would function as designed. This dichotomy is especially visible now, as appropriate reductions in nuclear stockpiles raise questions on the part of allies as to whether the US "nuclear umbrella" will remain large and strong enough to shelter them or whether they need to begin to think of creating their own nuclear capabilities, raising the specter of a dramatic increase in nuclear proliferation.

An additional and equally important consideration linked to the deterrence dichotomy is sustaining the quality of the human side of the nation's nuclear forces as the geopolitical environment changes, as nuclear deterrent capabilities lose some of their relevance and are replaced by advanced conventional arms, precision strike capabilities, and even cyber-weapons, and as proposals are considered for further drawdowns, including total elimination of nuclear weapons. How does one attract and retain high-quality, motivated personnel and sustain an uncompromising focus on safety, security, and integrity when the career path is increasingly viewed as no longer strongly linked to current threats and the needs of the nation? The need for sustained excellence rather than minimum compliance in the field is unarguable, but so is the human need of those who lead and follow to be a part of something significant and valuable to the nation. An organizational malaise, evidenced in operational errors, cheating scandals, or retention shortfalls, while perhaps understandable, is simply unacceptable. How the leadership deals with this dilemma is critically important.

Next is *Ethics*. Again, this implies that all participants in a conflict consistently hold a set of norms, standards, and expectations if an even-handed evaluation of ethical behavior in war is to be conducted in decision-making *in bello* or in a court of law or public opinion *post bellum*. The reality, again, is that such norms of behavior differ widely, not just between adversaries but among allies, as well. The aspiration for a universal standard is unlikely to be realized. But perhaps, as the poet said, "Ah, but a man's reach should exceed his grasp, Or what's a heaven for?"[6] Efforts in the United Nations toward international agreement have had some limited value in ascribing legitimacy to the use of armed force but are subject to partisan veto; international judicial tribunals have brought a level of post-conflict justice, but to only a senior few. Former secretary of defense Jim Schlesinger once noted to the author, "If a problem has no solution then it is no longer a problem, it is a fact and you have to deal with it." If a universal standard or code is likely unachievable and there is no agreement on what constitutes a "legitimate authority," then one could ask if we live in a world where we must either do what we and our allies think is right or accept that the evidentiary standards of the court of public opinion are now the norm and risk "crowd-sourcing" our ethical decision-making.

A second ethical consideration that has been partially prompted by the technology of weapons of mass destruction is the issue of preemption. In an age when a small group can now kill on an industrial level, can a preemptive strike be viewed as an ethical imperative? Andrei Sakharov devoted most of his professional life as a physicist to creating and then ensuring parity of force between the protagonists in a bipolar world dominated by two superpowers. In today's world, it can be inferred that one reason for the acquisition of a nuclear capability by states that do not possess it is an effort to provide a level of deterrence against potential preemption. The irony is that a situation can, therefore, be created where, as in a "do loop," a state must consider preemption in order to prevent the acquisition of a capability intended to foreclose that same preemption. In addition to countering the emergence of possible immediate and horrific threats, preemption has recently gained international support in the context of humanitarian intervention. The concept of "responsibility to protect" (R2P) argues that a state that is guilty of atrocities or genocidal policies forfeits its sovereignty and legitimacy and the international community has an obligation to intervene, by force, if necessary. The conflict in Kosovo is often cited as a successful example. How the concepts of R2P apply in non-state ethnic or religious conflict is less clear and, once again, raises the question of whose standards or criteria can be consistently applied, especially if we are trying to differentiate preemption from R2P.

A final ethical consideration involves the relationship between ethics and morals. As a general understanding, ethics are defined as widely shared societal or social norms, often codified, while morals represent a personal compass of principles or habits defining right or wrong. If intended to address behavior across the full spectrum of conflict participants, a review of ethics would seem incomplete without a consideration of the overlap of organizational or societal ethics with personal morality and how to address the tensions when the two do not precisely align. Sakharov said: "Life in its causes and connections is so complex that pragmatic criteria are often useless, leaving only the moral ones." To his biographer, this meant that "the moral criteria are not imposed from outside: it is his inner voice, his moral intuition."[7]

The word *Technology* is not particularly ambiguous, but as Sakharov noted and as quoted above, one needs to look beyond the technology to the underlying causes of tension, crisis, and war. This is not to imply that technology has not changed the scale and scope of the horrors of war—that is unarguable. It is also true that "step functions" in technology such as nuclear weapons, antiballistic missile defense, and offensive and defensive cyber-capabilities will always force us to think differently about how we approach conflict, from the strategic to the tactical. But technology has also brought significant benefits, partly by discouraging global conflict. Also, in a tactical context, improvements in weapon accuracy, nodal analysis, and intelligence collection have enabled less collateral damage, preservation of critical infrastructure, and more precise targeting of enemy combatants, reducing the level of civilian casualties. We should not be led to believe, however, that technological advances will render war obsolete. General Douglas MacArthur, in his storied farewell address at West Point over fifty years ago, opined, "Only the dead have seen the end of war."[8] While that remains a sad commentary on the human condition, history has yet to prove him wrong. For example, early in his career Sakharov had a self-described naïve belief in the compelling character of advancing technology. Though he had long concluded that needless atmospheric nuclear testing posed a real radiation threat to all mankind, he hoped that the detonation by the USSR of the largest hydrogen bomb ever built, in 1961, would lead both sides to see the folly of escalating levels of atmospheric nuclear testing. Instead, the United States abandoned its self-imposed moratorium within two weeks. Over the next year, both sides detonated over two hundred explosions, creating vast amounts of poisonous radioactive fallout. Intent versus effect in this case reminds us of the potential for manifestly different and wholly contrary results when attempting a purely linear linkage between cause and effect.

It is true that advances in technology have made some dimensions of warfare more impersonal and remote. The much-discussed advent of armed drones, long-range precision guided munitions, and cyberwarfare capabilities have caused some to ask if the lack of personal involvement in what has become, in some cases, a "video game war" has made it easier to use these capabilities absent a real sense of their impact. Interesting recent studies of drone operators have failed to corroborate this view, finding, instead, that the days of video observation that often precede a drone strike create a very personal linkage with the target on the part of the drone operator, actually increasing the emotional impact of the ultimately fatal attack.[9] In any case, further studies on this, as well as the relationship of the military to the society it serves cited above, are appropriate before drawing broad conclusions. Meanwhile, it is important to note that, despite new technology, close-quarter battle by our infantry sees a continuation of age-old tactics similar to those employed in centuries past. Such are the polarities of our current world.

Another aspect of technology that has brought new dimensions to decision-making in crisis and conflict is the arrival of the information age and the flood of information in which we are now awash. Logic would tell us that more is better as we struggle to move down the continuum from data to information to knowledge and, finally, to wisdom. Here, too, we can see both pros and cons. Commanders have access to intelligence, imagery, and analytical tools that can dramatically enhance situational awareness and subsequent ethical decision-making. There are certainly benefits to the networked battlefield where critical information can be quickly pushed to the level of the "strategic corporal" where it can have immediate tactical impact. But it is also true that possession of more data does not necessarily imply more certainty and, indeed, a command center filled with screens that offer what is sometimes termed the "God's-eye view" can lead the commander to believe he has "perfect" intelligence when he in fact has no way to display the "unknown unknowns" which must also inform his judgment. If we are affected by personal and organizational biases as well as bureaucratic processes, then applying more computing power just risks giving us the wrong answer faster. Even with the wonders of the information age, our search for wisdom remains as challenging as ever.

Another element of information flow that can affect ethical behavior in time of conflict is the speed with which information flows and the lack of a commensurate ability to rapidly separate truth from fiction or perception from reality. An English clergyman is supposed to have observed, "A lie can be halfway around the world before the truth gets its boots on."[10] In a sense, the time-constants of the world have all changed: pictures of atrocities appear globally minutes after they may or may not have happened and the demand for immediate action can shrink the time available for verification or a more dispassionate analysis of the long-term consequences. Disinformation, long a wartime reality in the guise of propaganda, can now fuel popular uprisings and encourage virulent nationalism. Even accurate information, now so rapidly available from around the globe, can sway popular opinion quickly, create perceptions, and pressure leaders to act without a complete understanding of the second- or third-order consequences.

A final aspect of technology with which we are only beginning to come to grips as a society is the incredible improvement in battlefield medical care. It is among the wounded that we see the most dramatic change in the character and challenges of combat. These challenges, too, have ethical and moral dimensions.

Dr. Atul Gawande, a Stanford-educated and Harvard-trained surgeon, has studied battlefield medical care. He points out that, though the firepower of combat has increased, the mortality has actually decreased dramatically in recent conflicts as a result of modern trauma care. "In the Revolutionary War," he says, "American soldiers faced bayonets and single-shot rifles, and 42 percent of the battle-wounded died. In World War II, American soldiers were hit with grenades, shells, bombs, and machine guns, yet only 30 percent of the wounded died. Over the next half-century, we saw little further progress. The casualty rate in both Vietnam and the Gulf War was 24 percent. Now the Army has brought modern mobile hospitals to the combat zone, a sort of MASH on steroids, and soldiers are often treated in minutes using modern techniques and are often back in a Stateside hospital in 36 hours receiving the finest medical trauma care in the world."[11] While the death of a single soldier brings a sadness beyond all telling, the fatality rate in the current conflict is now 10 percent.

This progress is wonderful, but it brings an ironic challenge. This sequence of care is unprecedented, and so is the result. Soldiers are receiving the gift of life with injuries that were not survivable in previous wars. We have never faced having to rehabilitate people with such extensive wounds. We are only beginning to learn what to do to make a life worth living for them. This challenge is a national and, yes, ethical responsibility, one that we all share. We must do all we can, not out of pity but out of gratitude and compassion. We must do more and they deserve no less. As Winston Churchill is supposed to have said, "It is not enough to do our best. We have to do what is required."

The final word for consideration in our title is *War*. Here, too, there are widely varying interpretations and definitions. Though the United States last declared war on December 8, 1941, the second half of the twentieth century and the first decades of the twenty-first have seen dozens of wars, both hot and cold, and countless situations where the difference between the two was largely a matter of semantics. From color revolutions to the Arab Spring and from classic nation-state confrontations to regional ethnic and religious conflicts that transcend or ignore national borders, the scale of war varies widely as do the principles of legal and ethical behavior that are applied. Classical study of ethics in combat, the "just war," tends to divide the review into phases: *jus ad bellum, jus in bello, and jus post bellum*. These are roughly parallel to the phases into which classic American military planning divides the task; one could legitimately ask whether this neat categorization, with its inferred differences in standards, is any longer appropriate. While not every conflict models Krulak's "Three Block War,"[12] with full-scale military action, peacekeeping, and humanitarian aid being conducted simultaneously by the same forces at the same time, the long-term conflicts in Iraq and Afghanistan have again blurred the lines between "in" and "after" war. In the glaring light of hindsight, we can see that those conflicts would have benefited from consideration thoroughly during the march *to* war of the full range of possible outcomes that we would need to deal with *after* the war. There is no alternative if we accept that the legitimate outcome of a just war must be a better peace.

This leads us, in summation, to a discussion of the role of strategy in ethical decision-making or, conversely, the importance of ethics in the creation of a strategy. There is a clearly identifiable cycle to most conflicts, often involving waves of violence and counter-violence that both precede hostilities and continue after the guns have gone silent. The importance of strategy cannot be overstated; the author has been quoted as saying that tactical energy in a strategic vacuum is a recipe for disaster. Clearly, a strategy is a prerequisite for conflict but it must also be comprehensive in its scope and depth and realistic in its assessments. Conventional wars generally end in a post-combat, pre-reconciliation state; should a strategy not sufficiently address the road to reconciliation the outcome of this war will sow the seeds of the next.

A strategy has to clearly enunciate objectives or goals, especially political, if we are to avoid being trapped in a cycle of endless and senseless warfare. Political, social, cultural, historic, ethnic, and religious realities must be addressed without the "mirror imaging" that often ascribes our own values to others, be they friend or foe. The strategy must then match resources with reality and understand that capability does not equal capacity, especially over the long term. We have found unexpected and interconnected challenges in simultaneously attempting to defeat an insurgency, rebuild a nation, and create a democracy where none had ever existed.

Finally, a strategy must be capable of measuring the costs of the overall military undertaking, not merely in monetary but also in human terms. Held in the balance, how do the benefits of humanitarian intervention, overthrow of a despotic regime, or preemption of weapons of mass destruction weigh against the societal, social, and security costs imposed on the populace? When the effort is complete and the effects are known, in the English expression, "will it be worth the candle?" This judgment, too, is an ethical responsibility of the nation's civilian leaders for which they are uniquely accountable. In addition to the ethical dimensions of the enterprise, it will generate a discussion and, one hopes, an understanding of the ethical and moral challenges likely to be faced by those who labor to carry it out by personal sacrifice in the dirt and dust of far-off places. If successful, we may yet achieve the vision of Andrei Sakharov, who hoped that "then, having overcome dangers and having achieved great development in all spheres of life, humanity will manage to keep the human in man."[13]

Notes

1. Gennady Gorelik and Antonina W. Bouis, *The World of Andrei Sakharov: A Russian Physicist's Path to Freedom* (New York: Oxford University Press, 2005).

2. Ibid.

3. Ibid.

4. Samuel B. Griffith, trans., *Mao Tse-tung on Guerilla Warfare* (New York: Praeger, 1961), 93.

5. Gorelik and Bouis, *The World of Andrei Sakharov.*

6. Robert Browning, "Andrea Del Sarto," in *The Complete Poetic and Dramatic Works of Robert Browning* (Boston: Houghton, Mifflin, 1895), 346.

7. Gorelik and Bouis, *The World of Andrei Sakharov.*

8. Douglas MacArthur, in his West Point speech on May 12, 1962, misattributed this remark to Plato, but it was originally from George Santayana's "Soliloquies in England," soliloquy no. 25, "Tipperary" (New York: Scribner's, 1924), 102.

9. James Dao, "Drone Pilots Are Found to Get Stress Disorders Much as Those in Combat Do," *New York Times,* February 22, 2013.

10. Attributed to Charles Haddon Spurgeon. "Sermons delivered in Exeter Hall, Strand, during the enlargement of New Park Street Chapel, Southmark" (1855).

11. Atul Gawande, *Better: A Surgeon's Notes on Performance* (New York: Henry Holt, 2007).

12. Charles Krulak, "The Three Block War: Fighting in Urban Areas," *Vital Speeches of the Day* 64, no. 5 (December 15, 1977): 139–41.

13. Gorelik and Bouis, *The World of Andrei Sakharov.*

A Military Perspective

Jim Mattis

We can better light our own path ahead by considering an approach to today's problems using the framework of a man who wrestled with the most fundamental ethical and moral issues of our time. The ethical issues inherent to military operations cut to the heart of what our democracies stand for. If the values that grew out of the Enlightenment are to be more than antique words in history books, those values must also guide our use of violence in defense of our freedoms. As such, ethics captured in the rules and regulations governing the conduct of our forces have long been embraced in our codes of conduct.

The paper submitted by my shipmate, Admiral Jim Ellis, brings the ethical framework into sharp focus, a focus that enables us to look critically at how a man like Andrei Sakharov might have addressed the complexities and ambiguities of battlefield forces.

In framing this issue we must marry our time: as Secretary Shultz has noted, our world is awash in change. Turmoil is currently characterizing increasing swaths of the globe; even islands of stability sense the impact of the violence more each day. Since 1979, the region with which I'm most familiar, the Middle East, has been engaged in multiple violent political arguments with barbarity spreading and hardening like a fast-growing cancer.

To guide us in such a world, we need anchor points if we're to remain authentic to the legacy we received from our Founding Fathers and to what a Nobel Peace Prize winner tried in his time to instill in a world that increasingly appeared to be losing faith in reason. This challenge brings to mind an old rock 'n' roll song from Crosby, Stills & Nash, one about teaching your children well. It includes the words, "You, who are on the road, must have a code that you can live by." Members of the military who engage in combat are on a "road" where passion and reason intersect and play with our moral sensibilities.

You will hear from some that in war you practice ethical conduct only at the expense of combat efficiency. Put differently, you can be fully effective in war only if you dismiss ethical restraints. Yet I have been to war repeatedly and never found ethics to restrain me in our efforts to defeat our enemies. Rather, an ethical foundation provides important guidance in developing our strategies and operational choices. In fact, history teaches us that either/or approaches to ethical issues can often bring a false premise and carry with them a false choice. For America has the power of inspiration as well as the power of intimidation. There is a human connection with morality and we deny that reality at our own peril. While not universally shared, that connection remains a source of real power.

As Alexis de Tocqueville intimated long ago, America will be a great country so long as it remains a good country, and should we cease to be good, we'll cease to be great. One of our military's lessons learned (or re-learned) over this last decade of war is that we must integrate and use *all* our national power in defense of freedom. By "all," we must include our moral power: we should never surrender the moral high ground, whether in policy or in military orders. While pragmatic approaches will be necessary, abandoning moral and ethical principles is unwise and will lessen our ability to win.

If we consider that premise, it follows that our military leaders need to align our military operations with America's legal principles. How else can our citizens reconcile war's grim realities with human aspirations? And absent such a reconciliation, how can we gain our countrymen's and women's support through the trials and tribulations that war's unpredictable nature will bring? Wartime passions will search for chinks in our spiritual armor, so whatever we do to strengthen our free society's belief in the moral purpose of our cause can only buttress our support when the tragedies of war come to bear.

In war, our soldiers, sailors, airmen, coast guardsmen, and Marines act in our countrymen's behalf and are accountable to our nation. Tied firmly to our nation's principles, we strengthen the bond that must exist between a democratic people and its military, a bond eroded since we shifted to a smaller, all-volunteer force. Those principles are the ones that grew out of the Reformation and the Enlightenment and were given voice in our founding documents. They are the same principles which give hope to oppressed people today and to those who can rally to us when crises strike. So surrendering those principles for some imagined short-term benefit is nonsensical from a geopolitical or enduring-combat-efficiency perspective.

In this role of examining our policymaking or of making military operational decisions, we are custodians of a legacy: we make choices, we are not victims, and we don't just follow orders—abrogating all moral responsibilities. Ethics and morality, defined appropriately in Admiral Ellis's paper (chapter 8), dictate that we must impose reason over impulse, especially when war's excesses can strip from each of us the veneer of civilization.

It's helpful to put this issue into its relevant historical context. Holding fast to a moral stance in the face of war's passions is not new, nor is it post-Vietnam-era legalistic political correctness run amuck. In April 1863, in the midst of the worst war in our country's history in terms of the numbers of Americans killed, United States General Orders [*sic*] no. 100 said in part, "Men who take up arms . . . do not cease on this account to be moral beings responsible to one another and to God." After years of carnage, President Abraham Lincoln and the US Army knew a thing or two about war's bloody realities, so this 150-year-old order cannot be dismissed as mindless blather out of touch with war's grim nature. The order made clear that we should not and would not give ourselves a moral pass even in the face of such terrible bloodletting.

This is hard work. Today, we confront foes who seek to reduce our military effectiveness by fighting from among noncombatants or even hiding literally behind the skirts of women. We see our enemies trying to use our moral stance and our ethical approach to war-fighting against us, all the while opening the aperture apocalyptically for whom they intentionally target or for whom they show callous disregard: the innocent noncombatants, including women and children. Our troops face severe challenges in carrying out their missions while holding fast to the moral high ground when the enemy, by firing from close proximity to the innocent, intentionally draws our fire on noncombatants.

In this circumstance we must remain steadfast in what we stand for. Just as importantly, we must be clear about what we will not tolerate from our own troops, because by discriminating our war-fighting approach from that of the enemy's we demonstrate better than any press release what we stand for. In achieving war aims, the moral is more powerful than the physical.

Again, this is hard work. Sakharov's vision notwithstanding, a universal human standard of conduct in the practice of violence has not been achieved and we must not delude ourselves: recent events have shown a level of barbarism that would excuse even the most heinous behavior if we were to allow the enemy dominion over our own military's ethical standards. But if today's medieval enemy is comfortable killing the innocent on an industrial scale in today's wars "among the people," we can make both moral and strategic arguments for adhering to our traditional ethical stance.

Take the case of infantry in close combat, an environment where atavistic behavior and intimate killing characterize young men's activities at the point of contact. Here we find war at its most primitive. Oliver Wendell Holmes Jr., a former Civil War infantry officer who rose to be a justice in our Supreme Court, said he and his fellow infantry veterans had "shared an incommunicable experience." If one of the most articulate justices in the history of the court could not put that combat experience into words, those who have not engaged in close combat will understand the near impossibility of any veteran doing so. Yet while that experience of real war is difficult to communicate, the broader requirement of our military to protect our country is not difficult to comprehend. And protecting our country includes protecting its honor as well as protecting the spirits of the lads we ask to do bad things to protect this experiment we call simply "America."

The fact that keeping one's moral stance in war is difficult is an excuse that neither history nor our country's citizens will accept. While we don't expect the impossible, we do expect that training, military discipline, and ethical leadership will sustain our country's values. We don't expect perfection; but callous disregard for our nation's values is not forgiven because one wears a uniform.

If we accept that the strategic level of warfare is the highest level, then tactical success in the absence of sound strategy will most often be found inadequate to achieving our purpose of war. Thus defining a sound strategic purpose for war is the critical first step in setting a moral stance. Even then it is sometimes difficult for militaries to understand that a tactically undefeated army can itself cause a war to be lost. Notably, in the information age, one way a country can win battles yet lose a war is through loss of the moral high ground, which can have the unintended effect of undercutting the strategic rationale for a war, no matter how morally right the decision was to go to war.

History also makes clear that countries with strong, committed allies generally defeat countries without allies. Our country will not hold the military advantages gained by the blood, sweat, and tears of our troops—specifically, we will not hold to our cause the allies who share our values and whom we need at our side—if we cannot hold the ethical high ground on which our strategic advantage rests. So our military operations must demonstrate ethical efforts if we're going to achieve the strategic advantage of holding allies close. For allies can help deter war as well as help carry war's burdens and end war swiftly and victoriously if we must fight. At the same time, should the enemy violate ethical or moral standards, this must be seen for the vulnerability it is; in this event, we should do everything in our power to use the enemies' acts against them in every venue, building an even stronger countervailing force to defeat them. When the enemy meets our troops on the battlefield, it must be the enemy's longest day and its worst day, for that success will help bind our allies to us. But battlefield skill and ferocity need not come at the expense of the moral high ground.

In my experience, in order to groom our military leaders to embrace, to live by, and to persuasively gain moral behavior by their troops, and to employ tactics that are ethically sound, we need physically tough leaders who employ a coaching or transformational style of leadership. Alternatively, the transactional style of command (one that is based on an enlistment "contract" or on tangible inducements to fight) is less compelling and will fail when such superficial aspects are laid bare on the battlefield and survival is in question. The coaching approach is more successful in drawing to service those who wish to better their character and to commit to something larger than themselves. The transformational approach is also better for returning veterans to society stronger for their experiences, proud of their service. Thus the father-son, teacher-scholar, or coach-player relationship in leadership is most likely to gain ethical adherence to something larger than a mere enlistment contract—which is ultimately just a piece of paper. Military training and discipline will have the best basis to take root when the conditions are set for their success by the admired, transformational-type leader. Lastly, admired leadership will gain more from subordinates in terms of valor and ethical performance than will threats of court-martial or jail.

Institutions, of course, get the behavior they reward, so we must ensure that we recognize and commend the military's ethical performance. When lapses occur they must be dealt with, and they will happen in wartime's unforgiving environment. As Geronimo noted, many bad things happen in war. Discriminating between mistakes made in the heat of battle and a lack of discipline is essential: we must maintain a sense of compassion for those in the fight who make mistakes (even when the results are tragic) while holding to account those who show a lack of self- or unit-discipline. Few things, however, can be more corrosive to maintaining high ethical standards than conflating mistakes with breaches of discipline: this will undermine ethical performance, create distrust in the ranks, and erode the legitimate ethical expectations our nation has come to expect from our military.

We are fortunate that our military has a legacy of moral military leadership on which to draw. From George Washington's decent treatment of British prisoners during our Revolution (despite the redcoats' abhorrent treatment of our captured men) to the Marshall Plan's approach for healing our former enemies' wounds after the bloodiest war in human history, we need only look to our past to find our better angels with answers that Andrei Sakharov would not have found wanting. History gives reassurance: after all, our predecessors faced worse yet they prevailed, keeping their honor clean despite uncertainties similar to what we face today.

Leadership is key, as noted above, when turning moral expectations into pragmatic guideposts for troops going into combat. Tough training of the young men we put into harm's way is critical, and leaders are responsible for setting up subordinate success by keeping training realistic. Troops know when their training has been tough, and the confidence developed by such training can help armor them for the ethical dilemmas sure to come. Such training creates a belief in themselves and in their leaders so long as those leaders are physically tough and have the persuasive force of personality to win their troops' affection as well as their trust. When leaders and led have a shared sense of co-equal commitment to the mission and to each other, then you have a unit most resilient and capable of holding its own, tactically and ethically. Weakly led units will often resort to cynicism on a host of issues. Cynicism is unmanly and reflects an abrogation of responsibility for one's actions because the cynic often sees his role as that of a victim. In an America where victimhood seems to convey high status, the military must not permit this response or we will find ready-made excuses for unethical behavior under the guise of salty cynicism.

Lapses in ethical performance can often be found in units that had physically soft leaders or leaders emotionally remote or psychologically removed from the realities of their subordinates. Any officer or headquarters that tries to play a role of referee between the enemy and our troops will quickly lose traction with subordinates; the rules of engagement must not be seen as tilting the battlefield to the enemy's advantage. Instead, by coaching troops to achieve harmony in combat operations (a vicious harmony as they close in on the enemy), we buttress them against misconduct when combat stresses strike. At the same time, we have no moral obligation to do the impossible and we should never assign such expectations to our military.

Legal training is a starting point, but it will not suffice in setting moral or ethical standards. What might be legal may yet be immoral, unethical, or plain counter-productive. "Legal" is a lesser standard and does not preclude stupidity or moral bankruptcy. While legal considerations will be considered in military operations to ensure our country remains true to its word given in international treaties, a more complete contextual framework is found in the rich literature of those who have gone before. Throughout history, similar ethical issues have found their way into conflict. The solutions practiced in history should be examined to help determine the best way ahead. There is no reason to not take advantage of the lessons learned over the last five thousand years of fighting on this planet.

In 1950, the United Kingdom contingent commander taking his troops to fight alongside the United States in Korea received a one-sentence order: "Do what is in the best interests of the Queen." Put into an American context, doing what is in the best interest of our country certainly precludes bringing dishonor on our nation. Leaders would do well to keep this in mind in the same way that leadership is inculcated in our military to "first do no harm." Our officers and noncommissioned officers are bred to be accountable to the American people for the ethical performance of those entrusted to their command. While any human organization has failures, those failures today are held to account and they do not define the US military. This is due to the eye-wateringly high quality of our troops, officer and enlisted, and the strong legacy of principled application of violence.

The US military is the gold standard of the world's militaries. Widely admired today by the American people and farther afield, it nonetheless faces the enduring challenges of adapting to a world awash in change. By holding fast to our hard-earned traditions and America's best values, even those that some may see as quaint or old-fashioned, we can best protect our country's future. The health of this national treasure called the US military, vital as it is to protecting this country, is dependent on maintaining its moral authority, an issue wholly in keeping with America's values.

Moral Reasoning and Practical Purpose

David Holloway

In the spring of 1974, Andrei Sakharov wrote a short essay for the American magazine *Saturday Review,* "The World in Half a Century." The opening sentences are as relevant today as they were forty years ago:

> Everyone who starts to think about the future of the world after fifty years—about that future in which our grandchildren and great-grandchildren will live—is seized by powerful and contradictory feelings. These are despondency and terror before the tangle of tragic dangers and difficulties in the immeasurably complex future of the human race, but at the same time hope in the power of reason and humanity in the souls of billions of people, which alone can resist the approaching chaos. The multifaceted and irrepressible scientific and technological progress of modern times also evokes a feeling of admiration and the liveliest interest.[1]

Sakharov was a theoretical physicist, but the relationship between technology and broader social and political purposes was central to his life and work. His understanding of that relationship changed over time in ways that are worth reflecting on as we think about the challenges we face today.

Thermonuclear Weapons and the Responsibility of the Scientist

Sakharov joined the Soviet nuclear project in 1948 at the age of twenty-seven. From 1950 to 1968 he worked at Arzamas-16 (the Soviet Los Alamos), where he played a key role in the development of thermonuclear weapons. He believed that the Soviet Union needed nuclear weapons of its own to balance the nuclear weapons of the United States and that, besides, it was not safe for the world to have just one nuclear-weapon state.

In November 1955 the Soviet Union tested its first two-stage thermonuclear weapon, in whose design Sakharov had played a leading role. This was a turning point in his life. He later recalled that witnessing the destruction caused by the explosion had triggered "an irrational yet very strong emotional impact. How not to start thinking of one's responsibility at this point?"[2] Here I want to focus on two occasions when he tried to alter Soviet policy with respect to nuclear weapons.

Banning Nuclear Tests

In 1957 Sakharov wrote an article titled "Radioactive Carbon in Nuclear Explosions and Non-threshold Biological Effects." The purpose of the article was to show that even "clean" nuclear bombs of the kind proposed by American physicist Edward Teller would have harmful biological effects. The "number of victims of additional radiation," Sakharov wrote, "is determined by non-threshold biological effects" such as carcinogenesis and genetic change. Large numbers of deaths and cases of disease could result. He calculated that the number of victims of a one-megaton detonation was ten thousand over a period of eight thousand years. Since, by his estimate, the total power of the bombs already tested was about fifty megatons, the number of casualties from those tests would amount to about five hundred thousand over that time. The article was published in the scientific journal *Atomnaia Energiia* (Atomic Energy) in 1958, with Soviet leader Nikita Khrushchev's permission.[3]

At the end of March 1958, the Soviet Union announced a unilateral moratorium on nuclear tests. This did not last long, however, for Khrushchev decided to start testing again on September 30. When Sakharov learned of this he sought to head off the resumption of tests. He prepared a proposal in which he argued that the Soviet Union should: continue the moratorium for another year; redesign the devices scheduled for testing so that they could be deployed without testing; renounce the doctrine that no device could be deployed without testing; invest heavily in computers and make more use of computer simulations in place of tests; and develop new experimental methods for modeling various functions of devices without full-scale testing. He went to Moscow to see Igor Kurchatov, scientific director of the whole Soviet project, who supported his idea. Kurchatov flew down to Yalta on the following day to talk to Khrushchev, who rejected Sakharov's proposal. The Soviet Union resumed testing on September 30, 1958, and conducted twenty tests before the three nuclear powers agreed at the end of October on a one-year test moratorium.[4]

This moratorium lasted almost three years, until September 1, 1961, apart from four test explosions conducted by France in that period. In the summer of 1961, at the height of the Berlin crisis, Khrushchev decided to end it. He told the Chinese foreign minister, Chen Yi, on July 5 that nuclear testing would be a "good method of pressure on the West."[5] On July 10 he informed a hastily convened meeting of leading nuclear scientists that testing would restart. Sakharov sent a note to Khrushchev during the meeting urging him not to resume testing. This provoked an angry response from Khrushchev:

Sakharov . . . has moved beyond science into politics. Here he's poking his nose where it doesn't belong. You can be a good scientist without understanding a thing about politics. Politics is like the old joke about the two Jews traveling on a train. One asks the other: "So, where are you going?" "I'm going to Zhitomir."

"What a sly fox," thinks the first Jew. "I know he's really going to Zhitomir, but he told me Zhitomir so I'll think he's going to Zhmerinka."

Leave politics to us—we're the specialists. You make your bombs and test them, and we won't interfere with you; we'll help you. But remember, we have to conduct our policies from a position of strength.[6]

In the last four months of 1961 the Soviet Union conducted sixty nuclear test explosions including a test of the hundred-megaton bomb that Sakharov had helped to design. The design was altered for the test, so that the yield would be fifty megatons; that was still the most powerful nuclear test explosion ever.

Sakharov continued to work on the design of nuclear weapons while hoping that nuclear tests in the atmosphere could be brought to an end. Negotiations among the Soviet Union, the United States, and Britain on a comprehensive test ban had been going on since 1958, but progress was blocked by disagreement over the monitoring and verification of underground tests. The idea of a treaty banning all except underground tests had been suggested by the United States but rejected by the Soviet Union. In the spring of 1963 one of Sakharov's colleagues at Arzamas-16, Viktor Adamskii, drafted a letter to Khrushchev supporting a partial test ban. He discussed this with Sakharov, who traveled to Moscow to give the letter to Efim Slavsky, the minister of medium machine-building, who was responsible for the nuclear weapons industry. The letter evidently reached Khrushchev, who put forward the idea of a partial test ban as a Soviet proposal on July 2. The treaty was signed by the United States, the Soviet Union, and Britain on August 27, 1963.

Adamskii's letter advanced three arguments in favor of a partial test ban. First, atmospheric pollution and radioactive fallout resulted from tests in the atmosphere. Underground tests would not produce those effects and would not contaminate ground water if the test sites were well chosen. Second, underground explosions could be used only to improve low-yield weapons and for experiments of little military significance. (This judgment proved to be mistaken: it underestimated what tunnel-boring technology could achieve.) A partial ban would limit the spread of nuclear weapons because a country that did not already have nuclear weapons would be unable to develop modern nuclear weapons without tests in the atmosphere. Third, the possibility of using nuclear explosions for peaceful purposes was linked to underground tests, not to tests in the atmosphere. A comprehensive test ban would prevent the peaceful nuclear explosions, which had a very promising future in a number of different areas.

It is not clear which of these arguments, as opposed to other considerations, might have carried weight with Khrushchev, though Sakharov did receive word from Slavsky that his proposal had elicited great interest at the top. It appears that Sakharov's intervention was a timely one and contributed to the conclusion of the Limited Test Ban Treaty.[7]

An ABM Moratorium

By 1965–1967, Sakharov and most of his colleagues at Arzamas-16 had come to two conclusions about missile defense. The first was that development of an effective anti-ballistic-missile (ABM) system was impossible if the potential adversary had comparable military-technical and military-economic potential. That was because the adversary could always find a way to overcome an ABM defense at considerably less expense. The second was that investing large sums in ABM deployment was not only burdensome, but also dangerous, because if both sides had powerful ABM systems, that would raise the threshold of stability or, more simply, the threshold of mutual assured destruction: each side would need larger offensive forces in order to have an assured capability to retaliate.[8]

On July 21, 1967, Sakharov wrote to Politburo member Mikhail Suslov asking for permission to publish an article on missile defense in the widely read weekly *Literaturnaia Gazeta*. The article consisted of an interview Sakharov had given under the title "Scientists and the danger of nuclear war."[9] In his letter to Suslov, Sakharov referred to Prime Minister Alexei Kosygin's recent meeting with President Lyndon Johnson in Glassboro, New Jersey, where Johnson and Secretary of Defense Robert McNamara had pressed Kosygin to reach an agreement on limiting ABM systems in order to clear the way to negotiations on reducing offensive systems. Kosygin was completely unreceptive to this idea, arguing that missile defenses were designed to save lives and were not a cause of the arms race: defensive and offensive systems should be considered together.[10]

Referring to Kosygin's public comments, Sakharov noted in his letter to Suslov that there was nothing in the Soviet press specifically devoted to ABM; that was why he wanted to publish his interview. He made the point that "creating ABM defenses against massed attacks is not realistic, while for individual missiles it is difficult but possible." An ABM moratorium would "correspond to the fundamental interests of Soviet policy," adding that many of the leading scientists at Arzamas-16 shared this view. Because the Soviet Union had "a significantly smaller technical, economic and scientific potential than the United States," the two countries were compelled to take different approaches in their evaluations of offensive and defensive weapons. There existed a saturation effect with respect to offensive weapons, but that was not true of ABM defenses, where the outcome of the competition would be determined by the relationship of the technological and economic potentials of the two sides.

Because the Soviet Union was weaker, Sakharov argued, it would have to rely on offensive rather than defensive systems. By his calculation, defenses were three to ten times more expensive than the offensive systems needed to overwhelm them. It made sense therefore to take the Americans' interest in an ABM moratorium at face value "both in the sense of a real limitation of the arms race, in which we are more interested than the US, and in the propaganda sense, to strengthen the idea of peaceful coexistence." American work on an ABM system was very advanced, he noted, and there was solid technical backing for several systems, but there was as yet no effective solution to the problem of missile defense. Nevertheless, there was the possibility that the "period of approximate and unstable equilibrium," which had begun in 1957, would not last forever, that the equilibrium could be broken, and that the illusion might arise that it could be broken. "Would we really give up the chance of a general settlement while it exists?" he asked. Sakharov requested that his letter be shown to Kosygin and Leonid Brezhnev, General Secretary of the Party Central Committee, and that was apparently done. Suslov refused to allow Sakharov's article to be published.

In that article Sakharov made the point that the question of a moratorium on anti-missile defenses "belongs to the category of highly sensitive matters that are difficult to discuss openly, but it is more important than ever to begin such a discussion." Suslov's refusal to permit the publication of Sakharov's article had a double significance. Not only did it signify rejection of Sakharov's position on an ABM moratorium (though in effect the Soviet leadership came round to that position in early 1970), but it also made clear that the Party leadership would not permit public discussion of ABM.

Suslov's response was a setback because Sakharov was coming increasingly to the view that sound policies had to be based on open discussion. He expressed this view very clearly in the essay he wrote in the early months of 1968, "Reflections on Progress, Peaceful Coexistence, and Intellectual Freedom." In the opening paragraph, Sakharov stated that his views were formed in the milieu of the scientific-technical intelligentsia, which was very worried about the future of humankind. Their concern, he continued, was all the stronger because what he called "the scientific method of directing politics, economics, art, education, and military affairs" had not yet become a reality. What did he mean by the "scientific method" in this context? His answer: "We consider 'scientific' that method which is based on a profound study of facts, theories, views, presupposing unprejudiced and open discussion, which is dispassionate in its conclusions." In other words, Sakharov took science as the model of politics, of a politics grounded in reason.[11]

Looking to the Future

The year 1968 marked a turning point in Sakharov's life. When "Reflections" was published abroad, he was quickly removed from secret work. He was able to continue doing physics, though now his time was increasingly occupied with civic activities. He was willing to lend his enormous prestige as a three-time Hero of Socialist Labor and "father of the H-Bomb" (a label he disliked, but it nonetheless stuck) in support of those suffering from political repression. His engagement with human rights grew stronger after his meeting with Elena Bonner in 1970 and their marriage two years later.

In 1975 Sakharov was awarded the Nobel Peace Prize for his work for human rights. The title of his Nobel lecture, "Peace, Progress, Human Rights," indicates a broadening of his thinking.[12] In his 1968 essay he had seen intellectual freedom as crucial for progress—how else could we deal with environmental degradation and the danger of thermonuclear war? In his Nobel lecture he stressed the importance of human rights, naming over one hundred of the political prisoners being held in the Soviet Union. He also made the general point that peace, progress, and human rights were indissolubly linked. For progress to be beneficial and peace secure, human rights (freedom of conscience, freedom of assembly, freedom of expression, etc.) had to be protected.

"Progress is possible and innocuous only when it is subject to the control of reason," Sakharov said in his Nobel lecture. "The important problems involving environmental protection exemplify the role of public opinion, the open society, and freedom of conscience." Similarly, disarmament required trust between states, and trust would be possible only with greater openness in public life. In this context human rights were crucial, because only if human rights were guaranteed would the conditions exist for the open debate and discussion needed for the creation of an informed public opinion: a public opinion that could ground power in reason and ensure the openness that was essential for a secure world.

These same themes were reflected in Sakharov's 1974 essay "The World in Half a Century."[13] The essay is enthusiastic about scientific-technical progress. Sakharov advances a number of "futurological hypotheses," including the division of the world into working zones and conservation zones; much greater use of cybernetic technology in industry; a world information system; a much greater role for computer modeling in the sciences; and economic exploitation of the moon. He notes also that abstract theoretical research can lead to very important and unexpected results. Scientific and technological progress is inevitable, in Sakharov's view. Only a general thermonuclear war, famine, epidemics, or general destruction could turn progress back—and one would have to be mad to wish for that.

But Sakharov's enthusiasm for science and technology is balanced by trepidation about the future. "Scientific-technical progress will not bring happiness," he writes, "if it is not complemented by extraordinarily profound changes in the social, moral, and cultural life of humankind. The most difficult thing to predict is the inner spiritual life of people, the inner impulses of their actions, but it is precisely on this that both the downfall and the salvation of civilization depend."[14] The most important unknown was the possible death of civilization and even of the human race in a thermonuclear war. If we avoided that, there were other ways in which the human race could perish: by exhausting its strength in "small wars" and international conflicts; by rivalry and by failure to agree in the economic sphere, in environmental protection, and in regulating population growth; and as a consequence of political adventurism. The human race was threatened by a decline in personal and state morality. This decline was manifest in the collapse in many countries of the ideals of law and legality, in consumer egoism, in the growth of criminal tendencies, in nationalist and political terrorism, in the destructive spread of alcoholism and drug-taking. The prime cause of these phenomena lay in an inner lack of spirituality and the resulting loss of a sense of personal morality and responsibility.

What could overcome these negative trends? Sakharov names several desirable changes in the world: overcoming the division of the world into antagonistic blocs through a process of convergence accompanied by demilitarization and the strengthening of international trust; defense of human rights, the law, and freedom; profound social progress and democratization; and the strengthening of the moral, spiritual and personal principle in human beings. The role of international organizations such as the United Nations and the United Nations Educational, Scientific, and Cultural Organization (UNESCO) ought to grow, ideally as the embryo of a world government. It was nevertheless important to take intermediate steps such as helping developing countries, especially in agriculture and in culture and spirituality, and creating consultative organs to monitor human rights and protection of the environment. The main thing, however, was human rights. "I want once more to emphasize that the struggle for human rights is today the real struggle for peace and the future of humankind," Sakharov wrote. "That is why I think that the Universal Declaration of Human Rights should be the basis for the activity of all international organizations including the United Nations, which adopted the Declaration twenty-five years ago."[15]

Moral Reasoning and Practical Purpose

No one who reads Sakharov's memoirs or his other writings can fail to be struck by the moral seriousness with which he approached the most important challenges facing the world. Some of the political changes he hoped for in his 1974 essay have come to pass—the end of the Cold War; greater activity by nongovernmental organizations (NGOs) on human rights and the environment; the spread of democracy. The world is much more open today than it was forty years ago. These changes have not always had the consequences Sakharov hoped for in terms of spirituality and morals, and we are still confronted by dangers of the kind Sakharov wrote about—nuclear war, climate change, epidemics, hunger, small wars—dangers that cannot be addressed by individual states alone and that require international cooperation.

In thinking about those dangers, three issues that Sakharov addressed are worth bearing in mind. The first is the relationship between science and politics. Sakharov wrote to political leaders recommending particular courses of action, but later came to the conclusion that that was not enough: there had to be public discussion and understanding of the issues. He shifted the focus away from the individual scientist's responsibility—important though that is—to the broader question of the world's capacity to cope with the great challenges that we face.

In reframing the issue, Sakharov underlined the importance of civil society and the public sphere. He developed a conception of politics based on the way in which science functioned: the state should be guided in its actions by civil society, or more specifically by a public opinion formed in the process of reasoned debate and discussion. In this conception of politics, the exercise of power is no longer the mere expression of the sovereign's will (in the Soviet case, the will of the Party leadership) but is grounded, like science, in reason. That kind of politics would be possible only in societies with strong protection for human rights.

When we think about the relationship between science and politics we should think not only about scientists and the state, but also about science oriented toward civil society and the broader public debates about the challenges we face. The key issue is then not the individual scientist's responsibility, but the scientific community's contribution to society's capacity to deal with those enormous challenges, many of which are, at least in part, the consequence of scientific and technological progress. How well organized are we to do this? And how best can this be done in a society in which the public sphere is changing rapidly as the result of the development of social media? Sakharov would surely have thought about the implications—both good and bad—of these new technologies for the defense of human rights.

The second issue relates to the first: the integrity of science and scientists. In drawing upon science as a model for politics, Sakharov was well aware that science did not always conform to the ideal: he had the example of the destruction of genetics (and geneticists) before him, and he spoke out against Trofim Lysenko and his attacks on genetics and geneticists.[16] But a less optimistic view of science can be found in Soviet dissident writings of the 1970s. Slanderer (*klevetnik*), a character in Aleksandr Zinoviev's satirical novel *The Yawning Heights,* expresses the view that careerism has created a "moral and psychological atmo-sphere in science which has nothing in common with those idyl-lic pictures one can find in the most critical and damning novels and memoirs devoted to the science of the past."[17]

The émigré science journalist Mark Popovsky painted a simi-lar picture, which Sakharov believed contained an important ele-ment of truth. Far from exercising a civilizing influence on Soviet society, science had come to embody the worst features of Soviet life: it was dominated by an overpowering bureaucratic appara-tus; careerism, patronage, and corruption were rife; there was a cynical disregard of ethics and morality; military and security considerations had first priority; and the scientific community was riven by national antagonisms and enmeshed in secrecy.[18] This raises questions that apply not only to the Soviet Union: How is science to maintain its integrity? How is it to maintain its authority, so that it can be effective in responding to the chal-lenges we face?

The third issue has to do with ethics. In his famous essay "Pol-itics as a Vocation," Max Weber drew a sharp distinction between an "ethics of principle" (*Gesinnungsethik*) and an "ethics of responsibility" (*Verantwortungsethik*). "There is a profound con-trast," he wrote, "between conduct that follows the maxim of an ethics of principle—that is, in religious terms, 'The Christian does the right thing and leaves the results to the Lord'—and conduct that follows the maxim of an ethics of responsibility, in which case one has to give an account of the foreseeable results of one's action."[19] Politics, in Weber's view, is the sphere in which the ethics of responsibility has to play a role, because politicians have to make judgments about the consequences of their actions. But once we start to consider the consequences of our actions we confront the question of means and ends.

Weber makes the argument:

No ethics in the world can dodge the fact that in numerous instances the attainment of "good" ends is bound to the fact that one must be willing to pay the price of using morally dubious means or at least dangerous ones—and facing the possibility or even the probability of evil ramifications. From no ethics in the world can it be concluded when and to what extent the ethically good purpose "justifies" the ethically dangerous means and ramifications.[20]

This, in Weber's view, is what gives to politics its particularly tragic character. The politician focuses on the end—the purpose—and may employ dubious means to attain that end. One good example of this is surely nuclear deterrence. During the Cold War all the nuclear powers adopted a policy of deterrence in one form or another: they wanted to avoid a new world war and they believed they could best do that by acquiring the capacity to retaliate in a devastating way against any state that attacked them. The goal of avoiding war was a good one; the means for achieving that goal—building up nuclear forces, training soldiers, airmen, and sailors to deliver nuclear weapons, choosing targets, writing computer code, and in general threatening to kill millions of people—were (and are) morally repellent.

There is no evidence that Sakharov ever read Max Weber, but he did face the ethical questions that Weber raises. In working to develop nuclear weapons—including the most destructive weapon ever built—Sakharov believed that he was helping to prevent nuclear war. This was surely an example of what Weber had in mind when he wrote of politicians using morally dubious means in the pursuit of a good end. Sakharov never regretted working on nuclear weapons, even when he became deeply critical of the Soviet state. He did, however, work to mitigate the harmful consequences of nuclear weapons development by lobbying for the cessation of nuclear tests and by drawing the Soviet leaders' attention to the destabilizing effects of ballistic missile defenses.

In his struggle for human rights, however, Sakharov adopted a principle closer to Weber's "ethics of principle." A Swedish journalist asked him in 1973, "You are doubtful that anything in general can be done to improve the system of the Soviet Union, yet you yourself go ahead acting, writing declarations, protests— why?" Sakharov gave an answer that stressed the importance of ideals as the basis for hope: "Well, there is a need to create ideals even when you can't see any route by which to achieve them, because if there are no ideals then there can be no hope and then one would be completely in the dark, in a hopeless blind alley."[21] Years later he wrote in his memoirs: "Life's causal connections appear so abstruse that pragmatic criteria are often useless; we must rely on our moral code."[22]

Conclusion

Sakharov's life serves as an inspiring example of the courageous application of moral reasoning to global challenges. His ideas serve as a guide to action. This is particularly true of the connection he drew between the human rights of each individual, the open society, and our capacity, as the human race, to deal with the great dangers and difficulties that confront us.

Notes

1. A. D. Sakharov, "Mir cherez polveka," in *Akademik A.D. Sakharov: Nauchnye Trudy* (Moscow: AOZT "Izdatel'stvo TsentrKom," 1995).

2. "Ia pytalsia na urovne svoei sud'by," interview with A. D. Sakharov, *Molodezh Estonii,* October 11, 1988.

3. "Radioaktivnyi uglerod iadernykh vzryvov i neporogovye bio-logicheskie effekty,"*Atomnaia energiia* 4 (1958): 576. See chapter 14 of Sakharov's memoirs on this episode and on Khrushchev's approval of the article's publication: Andrei Sakharov, *Memoirs* (New York: Alfred A. Knopf, 1990).

4. Sakharov, *Memoirs,* 205–9.

5. "Zapis' besedy N.S. Khrushcheva s ministrom inostrannykh del KNR Chen Yi," *Venskii val's kholodnoi voiny* (Moscow: ROSSPEN, 2011), 347.

6. Sakharov, *Memoirs,* 217.

7. On this episode see Sakharov, *Memoirs,* 230–32; V. B. Adamskii, "K istorii zakliucheniia moskovskogo dogovora o zapreshchenii iad-ernykh ispytanii v trekh sredakh," and Iu. N. Smirnov, R. M. Timerbaev, "K istorii zakliucheniia Moskovsogo dogovora 1963 goda o chastichnom zapreshchenii iadernykh ispytanii," in *Iz pokoleniia pobeditelei. Viktor Borisovich Adamskii. Izbrannye Trudy, vospominaniia* (Sarov: FGUP "RFIaTs-VNIIEF," 2008), 160–67, 576–97; and Viktor Adamskii, "Dear

Mr. Khrushchev," *Bulletin of the Atomic Scientists* (November/December 1995): 28–31.

8. Sakharov, *Memoirs*, 267–68.

9. Sakharov's article, "Scientists and the Danger of Nuclear War," can be found in *An End to Silence: Uncensored Opinion in the Soviet Union*, ed. Stephen E. Cohen (New York: W. W. Norton, 1982), 228–34. For the letter and the essay in Russian, see "Pis'mo Sakharova v Politburo TsK KPSS ot 21 iiulia 1967 goda," http://ggorelik.narod.ru/ADS68 /ADS_AMB_TsK_670721.htm. See also Gennady Gorelik and Antonina W. Bouis, *The World of Andrei Sakharov: A Russian Physicist's Path to Freedom* (New York: Oxford University Press, 2005), 263–70.

10. For a discussion of Kosygin's remarks, see Raymond L. Garthoff, "BMD and East-West Relations," in Ashton B. Carter and David N. Schwartz, eds., *Ballistic Missile Defense* (Washington DC: Brookings Institution, 1984), 295–97.

11. Andrei D. Sakharov, *Progress, Coexistence, and Intellectual Freedom* (London: Andre Deutsch, 1968), 25.

12. Andrei Sakharov, Nobel lecture, "Peace, Progress, Human Rights," http://www.nobelprize.org/nobel_prizes/peace/laureates/1975 /sakharov-lecture.html.

13. Sakharov, "Mir cherez polveka," n1.

14. Ibid., 401.

15. Ibid., 403.

16. Sakharov, *Memoirs*, chapter 17.

17. Aleksandr Zinoviev, *Ziiaushchie Vysoty* (Lausanne: L'Age d'Homme, 1976), 143.

18. Mark Popovsky, *Science in Chains: The Crisis of Science and Scientists in the Soviet Union Today* (London: Collins and Harvill Press, 1980).

19. Max Weber, "Politics as a Vocation," in *From Max Weber: Essays in Sociology*, ed. H. H. Gerth and C. Wright Mills (New York: Oxford University Press, 1946), 120. I have changed the standard translation here for *Gesinnungsethik* from "ethic of ultimate ends" to "ethics of principle," which seems to me to capture Weber's meaning more accurately.

20. Weber, "Politics as a Vocation," 121.

21. See "Interview with Olle Stenholm," in Sakharov, *Memoirs*, 627.

22. Sakharov, *Memoirs*, 561.

A Global Commons:
A Vision Whose Time Has Come

James E. Goodby

Andrei Sakharov's Glimpse into the Future

International relations and *international security* referred until very recently to the way humanity, represented by nation-states, organized its affairs in the vast realm external to each individual nation-state. Even advocates of world government were preoccupied with interstate conflicts and how to reduce anarchy in relations among states. Today, the nation-state is still the main engine of cooperation and conflict but many, if not all, of the existential threats faced by humanity are global in nature and cannot be managed except by a global response or, in some cases, a regional response. Andrei Sakharov, with his prophetic vision of how human society would evolve, saw this before almost anyone else.

Sakharov had a remarkable gift for discerning trends in human affairs. He foresaw that there would be major consequences from the changes beginning to pile up in his lifetime. He said civilization is imperiled by a thermonuclear war, mass famine, and the unforeseeable consequences of swift changes in the conditions of life on our planet. He asserted that the division of humanity would have to be overcome in order to avoid destruction. He sought a society that would care for the Earth and its future.[1]

And Today's Reality

Former Secretary of State George P. Shultz looks at today's world and often remarks that "the world is awash in change." He sees that national sovereignty has been eroded, that international institutions established after World War II, which exerted a powerful influence for decades, cannot cope with new global challenges. Accordingly, he sees the need for a "global commons." His conclusion in essence is similar to that of Sakharov: humanity divided cannot deal with the changes in the conditions of life on our planet.

What Is a Global Commons?

When I use the term *global commons,* I use it the way George Shultz uses it, in the sense that there are challenges that affect all humanity, and that humanity has a common interest in dealing with these issues. It is time for an international conversation about a new global commons. Thinking afresh about this means defining a global commons relevant to twenty-first-century needs. An emerging global society, which is the chief new characteristic of international life today, has a set of existential interests, and these interests can be thought of as the commons of a global society. Because of all the changes sweeping the globe, the sense of uncertainty and complexity is acute, with old dangers taking new unplanned shapes and new dangers not yet well understood. This calls out for a serious rethinking about many of our institutions and assumptions. A heightened sense of urgency and fresh perspectives on global challenges must be communicated by those most engaged in global problem-solving, as well as those who are the prime communicators of our time. The challenge is to identify and define the array of existential threats to humanity that establishes the need for nations to cooperate at the global level to avoid extinction, and then for nations to create mechanisms for carrying out order-building diplomacy that will permit society to build a global commons, that is, a management system to deal with common threats.

The Conditions of Life on Our Planet

Sakharov spoke of the swift changes in the conditions of life on our planet. Today, these changes include the following:[2]

Urbanization. Nearly all the nations of the world are becoming urbanized, which means that governance will have to be based on management of urban needs for housing, health care, education, and cultural assets. Empowerment of citizens living in cities is enhanced, despite some governments' efforts to stop it, by the inevitable spread of information technology. The combination of urbanization and instant information and communications resources by large masses of people should make leaders more accountable to the governed. It may also be the source of tensions, leading to repression.

Migration. The time is not far off when migration will be the result of climate change, which will deprive some regions of habitable conditions. Drought and rising sea levels will require massive resettlement of populations in affected areas. The challenge for governance is whether this can be managed in an orderly way, with the resilience that will be required of civil society. The economic consequences could be catastrophic and nations or regions that can best plan for relocation of people and jobs will be the winners.

Critical resources: water and food. The availability of water is a serious problem in some regions. Almost certainly it will get worse as climate change dries up the sources of water in some areas at a time of increasing demand for food by a growing population. Technology can address this and so can conservation measures, but time is running out.[3]

Areas where food production has been dependent on adequate sources of water may be deprived of any means of continuing an economy dependent on water. This will encourage migration;

large areas may fall victim to either desertification or to over-crowding as new waves of migration move into water-rich parts of the world. Shortages of water are not being met with anything like the level of resources and research that will be required in the future. Alternative sources of water on the scale that will be needed will be difficult to find and impossible to exploit without intergovernmental cooperation. Technologies for converting saltwater to potable water are available but scaling remains a problem. Recycling and conserving water could be achieved on a broader scale currently but national policies generally are not in place to have the effect that will be needed.

Energy. Energy is perhaps the one area where there are reasonably clear answers to the challenges the world faces. Fortunately, a sustained research program has been under way for several years, especially in the United States, in response to economic, security, and environmental concerns. This has given the world options that were not available just a decade or so ago.

Demand for energy is increasing as urbanization and improvements in living standards proceed, but new sources of energy and new methods of delivering electric power can keep up with the demand. The most difficult area for future cooperation is how rapidly carbon-based fuels can be phased out. Already, natural gas is displacing coal simply because of the economic advantages. Those issues present major challenges for governance but, thanks to major advances in the technology of energy, answers are available.

Systemic Change

All of these challenges to the well-being of humanity are made even more complex by the fact that ours is a time of unusually rapid change in human affairs. More than twenty years ago, a brilliant British-Australian scholar named Hedley Bull wrote a book called *The Anarchical Society*.[4] In it, he analyzed plausible alternatives to the state system as it stood at that time. His conclusion was that there were no plausible alternatives. Even terrorists who were attacking state institutions were simply trying to create their own states. If Bull were writing that book today, he would have to conclude that the positions of states in the international system are being challenged by other power centers within the emerging new system.

Bull described the structure of the pre-Westphalian international system.[5] It was a three-tiered system, in which there was a global norm-setting mechanism which wielded some power of its own. In medieval times in Europe that was the Church. Today, global institutions like the World Trade Organization, international financial organizations, and the United Nations set global norms. Second, there were the sovereigns, kings and queens desperately trying to gain and keep control of territories. Their sovereignty was limited from above by the Church and from below by powerful barons, who exercised a significant degree of sovereignty over their own turf. Today, if you look around you in Silicon Valley, you see exactly what I mean: large economic units—think Google and Apple—that exercise a form of sovereignty of their own.[6] So it seems to me we see emerging what amounts to a three-tiered power-sharing system, where the sovereign states are no longer in complete charge. That system is still evolving. It's very rudimentary at this point. Governments can still shape it if they understand what is happening.

There was a fourth element in Europe—the Holy Roman Empire. Today, we see the European Union in Europe. Regional organizations also exist in Latin America, Africa, the Middle East, and Central Asia. Nuclear-free zones exist in several parts of the world. There is a role emerging for regional organizations and these might outpace global organizations in their impact on the international system.

If megatrends like these are truly re-shaping the international system, governments ought to be thinking more strategically about where these megatrends are taking us. These trends are not fully within the control of national governments to manage but governments are still the major source of executive actions and can influence the course of events. If the world is moving in the direction that I've just described, what does that mean in terms of what we should be doing with respect to policy? It seems to me that, above all, it means that we should be thinking more seriously than we appear to be about the idea of the global commons.

Issues of Governance

If changes in the international system require power-sharing by governments with regions, global institutions, major urban centers, and economic organizations with global reach, then to govern effectively governments must create coalitions with these other power centers to a degree that is unprecedented during the past three hundred years. But many issues facing governments today impose that kind of approach, as Sakharov foresaw many years ago. A failure to govern in cooperation with these diverse power centers in an era when citizens and private organizations have the means to acquire and disseminate massive amounts of information and opinions almost instantaneously is a prescription for being bypassed by history.

Much more work is necessary to identify the kinds of power-sharing coalitions that will be an essential part of successful governance. But already it can be said that this will require a major change in the way various countries' policymakers view national security requirements. It will require plans and programs no less visionary than those ideas of the Western leaders in the late 1940s and '50s, which resulted in more than a half-century of non-war among the big powers of the world and significant economic development on a broad basis. Strategic foresight and political courage matching those of earlier times are now needed on the part of current and next-generation leaders. And this time, it will have to include leadership in all parts of the globe.[7]

Overcoming Divisions

One aspect to which Sakharov was very sensitive in this connection is the struggle between open and closed societies, between a nationalism that seeks to divide and a nationalism that is built on universal values and is inclusive in its approach to other nations. One type of nationalism discourages diversity; the other type welcomes it. One type is backward-looking; the other looks to the future.

What does this mean for those of us who cherish diversity and openness? Here, we can do no better than follow Sakharov's prescient advice:

> The division of mankind threatens it with destruction . . . any action increasing the division of mankind, any preaching of the incompatibility of world ideologies and nations is madness and a crime.[8]

Policies of inclusion—even in the face of rejection and derision from those who seek to divide—is the only way to a lasting peace. And what's more, the universal information system that Sakharov foresaw forty years ago—a system remarkably like today's Internet—puts policies of exclusion on the wrong side of history. Efforts to turn back the clock are unlikely to succeed.

Fragmentation occurs as a long-standing international system undergoes fundamental change. It's natural, as globalization proceeds, and you can see that almost everywhere. That's part of the change that is occurring within the international system right now. It's a fact of life governments have to deal with. Sometimes, it generates armed conflict. It may promote divisions among peoples.

What kinds of societies are best able to deal with that kind of a situation? I would argue that democracies are far better equipped to deal with this kind of a chaotic situation than totalitarian societies or authoritarian societies. This is why, I think, you see countries like Russia and China interested in territorial dominance, more so than countries in the West. They have few other ways of projecting power than through that means. And that is exactly why we have to think about how to deal with the issue of fragmentation and divisions in the global commons.

Alliances, I think, are appropriate for the regional part of the problem. Almost all alliances that the United States is involved in are in Europe, Northeast Asia, or the Western Hemisphere. I think we also need to concentrate on creating additional regional organizations in which the United States might be a facilitator, not necessarily a participant. I do not believe that at the global level alliances are appropriate. The existential threats I have described require global functional cooperation, but not alliances.

A Joint Nuclear Enterprise

One example of how to and how not to operate in the global security commons is the nuclear threat, where years of experience have provided many lessons. Perhaps the chief among them is that nuclear reductions and more cooperative international relationships go hand in hand. It is now clear, also, that the circle of nations actively engaged in major nuclear negotiations must be enlarged beyond Russia and the United States.

Sakharov well understood the dangers of nuclear deterrence and also understood that the dangers must be met by a joint enterprise. It is not clear that his deep concerns are as widely shared today as they should be. Persuading publics and parliaments that cooperative measures are necessary to reduce nuclear dangers is essential and the task will not be easy.

Today's security environment has made reliance on nuclear deterrence an even more risky business than in Sakharov's time. Consider what has happened since the end of the Cold War:

- Sub-state entities have shown themselves to be interested in and capable of inflicting mass casualties. If they could buy or steal a nuclear weapon, they would use it.
- India and Pakistan have built nuclear arsenals and have positioned their armed forces in a way that makes nuclear war between them a serious possibility.
- North Korea has built the infrastructure for a nuclear weapons program and there is little that prevents it from continuing to add nuclear weapons to its arsenal.
- The bipolar nuclear structure of the Cold War has been replaced by a complex structure distinguished by three global confrontations (China, Russia, and the United States) and

three intra-regional confrontations (the Middle East, South
Asia, and Northeast Asia). Opportunities for miscalculations
abound.
- Science and technology have produced new weapons systems,
including cyberwarfare and drones which make the practice
of nuclear deterrence even more risky than it was during the
Cold War. False signals difficult to trace and weapons too
small to easily detect will complicate a murky situation and
easily induce miscalculation.

How right Sakharov was when he said that "nuclear deterrence is
gradually turning into its own antithesis and becoming a dangerous remnant of the past."[9]

Nuclear weapons present the most vivid example of how interstate relations are influenced by military force: a stable peace cannot be achieved between two nations while nuclear competition
exists between them. In contrast, building cooperation between
two adversaries can alter perceptions of the wisdom of having
nuclear weapons. Existential issues common to the emerging
global society can more readily be solved in a world where the
nuclear status quo has been successfully challenged and a decisive
turn in international relationships has been made. This is what
began to happen in the 1980s under the leadership of Ronald
Reagan in the United States and Mikhail Gorbachev in the Soviet
Union. Recent events in the West's relations with Vladimir
Putin's government in Russia show how closely linked are political relations and nuclear cooperation.

An advantage of the nuclear project is that it also highlights
a number of unresolved international problems, some of them
regional, that would have to be addressed in creating the conditions for a world without nuclear weapons. It also makes possible
a more comprehensive approach that provides more confidence
and assurance of stability on many levels.

How could a joint nuclear enterprise open doors to the management of other existential global security challenges and so
enlarge the scope of the global security commons? This model
would have shown that it is a viable means of addressing global
security challenges: order-building diplomacy is key to managing

all the existential challenges that are part of the global security commons. Cooperation would have been shown to be superior to competition as a way of building the global security commons.

Summing Up

The global commons must be managed and sustained across generations in the interests of the whole of humanity. Nation-states remain the main engine for governing over such issues. With few exceptions, existing international institutions have not dealt with existential issues as these have arisen in recent decades. Coalitions of nations have struggled with global issues but not, in any sustained way, with existential security issues. Limited success, at best, even in the economic field, has been achieved by the G-8 and the G-20.

Cooperation among nations obviously has been hard to achieve. As mentioned above, regionalism is one potentially important form of cooperation but too often it is thought of as closed to outsiders—a way of maximizing national power, not as a contribution to a global commons. Existing organizations, institutions, and diplomatic paradigms have not been capable of showing that cooperation would serve the nations better than competition. But unrestrained competition—zero-sum games—inevitably bring bad outcomes and should constitute a standing incentive for changing the playing field.

What would it take to change this situation? It is easier to say it than to do it, but in the nuclear arena a grand design would include a summit-level commitment and a determined multiyear effort with clear goals. This should encourage public acceptance that a global commons successfully meets existential challenges that can only be met through cooperation at both the regional and the global level. Otherwise, as Sakharov said long ago, humanity will face destruction.

Notes

1. Andrei Sakharov, "Thoughts on Progress, Peaceful Coexistence and Intellectual Freedom," May 1968. Published in the *New York Times,*

July 22, 1968. Full text of the most relevant quotation is as follows: "The division of mankind threatens it with destruction. Civilization is imperiled by a universal thermonuclear war, catastrophic hunger for most of mankind, stupefaction from the narcotic of 'mass culture,' and bureaucratized dogmatism, a spreading of mass myths that put entire people and continents under the power of cruel and treacherous demagogues, and destruction or degeneration from the unforeseeable consequences of swift changes in the conditions of life on our planet."

2. This draws on discussions at "The Challenge of Governing over Diversity in an Age of Transparency," held at the Hoover Institution, Stanford, California, April 29–30, 2014, in cooperation with the Defense Department's Near East South Asia Center for Strategic Studies.

3. See Salman Masood, "Starved for Energy, Pakistan Braces for a Water Crisis," *New York Times,* February 12, 2015.

4. Hedley Bull, *The Anarchical Society: A Study of Order in World Politics,* 2nd ed. (New York: Columbia University Press, 1995).

5. Ibid., 245–46.

6. See David E. Sanger and Nicole Perlroth, "Obama Heads to Tech Security Talks amid Tensions," *New York Times,* February 12, 2015. The article speaks of "the deepening estrangement between Silicon Valley and the government."

7. See "US Allies, Lured by China's Bank," *New York Times,* editorial, March 20, 2015.

8. Sakharov, "Thoughts."

9. Andrei Sakharov, "Andrei Sakharov from Exile" (New York: International League for Human Rights, October 1983). Texts were written by Sakharov in exile in Gorky.

Conference Agenda:
Andrei Sakharov and the
Conscience of Humanity

December 10–11, 2014

Wednesday, December 10, 2014

8:15 a.m.   Breakfast

8:45 a.m.   Opening Remarks: George P. Shultz and
                  Sidney D. Drell

9:00 a.m.   *Session I: Introduction*

                  Serge Schmemann: The Evolution of Andrei
                  Sakharov's Thinking from Nuclear Weapons to
                  Human Rights, and His Emergence as a Coura-
                  geous Leader in Efforts to Reduce the Growing
                  Threats to Humanity

10:30 a.m.   Break

10:45 a.m.   *Session II: Humanitarian Issues*

                  J. Bryan Hehir: The Scientist as Prophet:
                  Sakharov's World and Ours
                  William Swing: The Soul and Sakharov

12:30 p.m.   Lunch *f*

1:30–5:00 p.m.   *Session III: Where Is Science Taking Us? Case Studies and Major New Developments*

                    Raymond Jeanloz: Environmental Effects of Nuclear War
                    Lucy Shapiro: Decoding the Biosphere and the Infectious Disease Threat
                    Elizabeth Holmes: Diagnosis Reinvented
                    Christopher Stubbs: The Sakharov Conditions, Disruptive Technologies, and Human Rights

6:00 p.m.   Reception and Archives Exhibition

7:00 p.m.   Dinner

Personal Reminiscences of Andrei Sakharov:
Tatiana Yankelevich and Sidney D. Drell

Thursday December 11, 2014

8:15 a.m.   Breakfast

8:45 a.m.   *Session IV: View of the Military on Ethical Issues and Strategic Choices in Dealing with Death and Destruction on an Unparalleled Scale; Use of Drones*

                    James O. Ellis Jr.: New Dilemmas in Ethics, Technology, and War: Sakharov's Principles in Today's World
                    Jim Mattis: A Military Perspective

10:30 a.m.   Break

10:45 a.m.   *Session V: Interplay of High Purpose with Reality in Efforts to Reduce the Growing Threats to Humanity*

George P. Shultz speaking at a symposium reviewing Andrei Sakharov's legacy in 1999, ten years after his death. Photo by Harvey Lynch.

David Holloway: Moral Reasoning and Practical Purpose

James E. Goodby: A Global Commons: A Vision Whose Time Has Come

12:30 p.m.   Lunch

1:30 p.m.   *Session VI: Governance in a World Awash in Change and with Diversity; The Importance of Leaders like Andrei Sakharov with the Vision and Courage to Act under Severe Conditions*

                  Jim Hoagland

Summing Up   **Sidney D. Drell and Jim Hoagland**

About the Participants

Gerhard Casper is president of the American Academy in Berlin and president emeritus of Stanford University. He is also the Peter and Helen Bing Professor, Emeritus, and a senior fellow at the Freeman Spogli Institute for International Studies at Stanford. Casper studied law at the universities of Freiburg, Hamburg, and Yale, and then returned to Freiburg, where he earned his doctorate in 1964. After an initial teaching position at the University of California, Berkeley, Casper was recruited two years later by the University of Chicago, where he spent twenty-six years, served as dean of the law school, and, in 1989, became provost, a post he held until he accepted the presidency of Stanford University in 1992. He has written and taught primarily in the fields of constitutional law, constitutional history, comparative law, and jurisprudence. His most recent book, *The Winds of Freedom: Addressing Challenges to the University,* was published by Yale University Press in February 2014.

Sidney D. Drell is a senior fellow at Stanford's Hoover Institution and a professor emeritus of theoretical physics at the SLAC National Accelerator Laboratory. For many years he has advised the US government on technical national security, arms control, and defense issues, including serving on the President's Foreign Intelligence Advisory Board and the President's Science Advisory Committee. His fundamental scientific research and his contributions to the government have been recognized by election to the National Academy of Sciences and by numerous awards, including the National Medal of Science, a prize fellowship from the MacArthur Foundation, and the National Intelligence Distinguished Service Medal. He is one of ten scientists honored as "founders of national reconnaissance as a space discipline" by the National Reconnaissance Office. He met Andrei Sakharov in 1974 and they became close friends, with Drell working to support Sakharov's courageous and passionate fight for human rights.

James O. Ellis Jr. is an Annenberg Distinguished Visiting Fellow at the Hoover Institution. He retired as president and chief executive officer of the Institute of Nuclear Power Operations, a self-regulatory nonprofit located in Atlanta, Georgia, in 2012. In 2004, he completed a thirty-nine-year US Navy career as commander of the United States Strategic Command. In this role, he was responsible for the global command and control of US strategic and space forces. His sea service included carrier-based tours with three fighter squadrons and command of the USS *Abraham Lincoln,* a nuclear-powered aircraft carrier. His shore assignments included commander in chief, US Naval Forces, Europe, and Allied Forces, Southern Europe, where he led United States and NATO forces in combat and humanitarian operations during the 1999 Kosovo crisis. He is a member of the National Academy of Engineering.

James E. Goodby is an Annenberg Distinguished Visiting Fellow at the Hoover Institution, Stanford University, where he works with former Secretary of State George Shultz and noted physicist Professor Sidney Drell. He is also affiliated with the Brookings Institution and the Massachusetts Institute of Technology. He served for over thirty years in the US Foreign Service and was given five presidential appointments to ambassadorial rank, including as US ambassador to Finland. He has written and edited numerous books and articles while teaching at Stanford, Georgetown, Syracuse, and Carnegie Mellon universities. He is a distinguished service professor emeritus at Carnegie Mellon.

J. Bryan Hehir is the Parker Gilbert Montgomery Professor of the Practice of Religion and Public Life at Harvard Kennedy School of Government. He previously served as president of Catholic Charities USA and was on the staff of the US Conference of Catholic Bishops, as well as serving on the faculty of the Georgetown School of Foreign Service.

Jim Hoagland is a two-time winner of the Pulitzer Prize for the *Washington Post,* where he is now a contributing editor. He joined the newspaper in 1966 and served as a reporter, editor, bureau chief for Africa, the Middle East, and Western Europe, senior foreign correspondent, and syndicated columnist. He is a graduate of the University of South Carolina and did graduate work at the University of Aix-en-Provence in France and at Columbia University in New York. He was a staff member of the *New York Times* international edition in Paris from 1964 to 1966. He won Pulitzer prizes in 1971 (international reporting) for a ten-part series on apartheid in South Africa and in 1991 (commentary) for opinion articles warning of Iraq's predatory intentions and showing how and why Mikhail Gorbachev's efforts to save communism and the Soviet state were doomed. He is an Annenberg Distinguished Visiting Fellow at the Hoover Institution.

David Holloway is the Raymond A. Spruance Professor of International History and a senior fellow at the Freeman Spogli Institute for International Studies at Stanford University. Among his publications is *Stalin and the Bomb: The Soviet Union and Atomic Energy, 1939–1956* (Yale University Press, 1994). His current research focuses on the international history of nuclear weapons.

Elizabeth Holmes is CEO of Theranos, which she founded in 2003 with the mission to make actionable health information accessible to people everywhere at the time it matters, enabling early detection and intervention of disease, and empowering individuals with information to live the lives they want to live. She attended Stanford University's School of Engineering before founding Theranos. She is a recipient of the 2015 Horatio Alger Award.

Raymond Jeanloz, a senior fellow in the Miller Institute for Basic Research in Science and a geophysics professor at the University of California, Berkeley, studies materials at high pressures. He is a long-standing adviser to the US government and the University of California in areas ranging from Earth science to national and international security and has written extensive technical analyses on topics related to nuclear weapons, international threats, and nonproliferation. He is an Annenberg Fellow at the Hoover Institution, serves on the Secretary of State's International Security Advisory Board, and chairs the National Academy of Sciences Committee on International Security and Arms Control.

Jim Mattis retired as a general after serving forty years as an infantry officer in the US Marine Corps. His final tours of duty included commander of US Joint Forces Command, supreme allied commander for NATO's transformation, and commander of US Central Command, during which he was responsible for American military operations throughout the Middle East. He serves today as an Annenberg Distinguished Visiting Fellow at Stanford University's Hoover Institution.

William J. Perry is the Michael and Barbara Berberian Professor (emeritus) at Stanford University. He is a senior fellow at the Freeman Spogli Institute for International Studies and serves as director of the Preventive Defense Project. He is an expert in US foreign policy, national security, and arms control. Perry served as secretary of defense from February 1994 to January 1997. He previously served as deputy secretary of defense (1993–1994) and as undersecretary of defense for research and engineering (1977–1981). He serves on the Defense Policy Board and International Security Advisory Board. He is on the board of directors of Theranos, Xyleco, and several emerging high-tech companies.

Serge Schmemann is a member of the editorial board of the *New York Times* based in Paris, focusing on international issues. He was for many years the *Times* bureau chief in Moscow, and was also posted to South Africa, Germany, Israel, and the United Nations. He was deputy foreign editor of the *Times* from 1999 to 2001. Schmemann was awarded a Pulitzer Prize in 1991 for coverage of the reunification of Germany and an Emmy in 2003 for his work on a television documentary about the Israeli-Palestinian conflict. He wrote *Echoes of a Native Land: Two Centuries of a Russian Village* (Vintage, 1997) and *When the Wall Came Down: The Berlin Wall and the Fall of Soviet Communism* (New York Times, 2006).

Lucy Shapiro is the Virginia and D. K. Ludwig Professor at Stanford University's School of Medicine and is the director of the Beckman Center for Molecular and Genetic Medicine. She founded the anti-infectives discovery company Anacor Pharmaceuticals and is a member of the Anacor board of directors. She has been the recipient of multiple honors, including election to the American Academy of Arts & Sciences, the National Academy of Sciences, the Institute of Medicine, and the American Philosophical Society. She was awarded the FASEB Excellence in Science Award, the Selman Waksman Award from the National Academy of Sciences, the Canada Gairdner International Award, the Abbott Lifetime Achievement Award, and the Horwitz Prize. President Obama awarded her the National Medal of Science in 2012.

Jane Shaw is Dean for Religious Life and a professor of religious studies at Stanford University. Before coming to Stanford in 2014, she was dean of Grace Cathedral in San Francisco for four years, and before that taught theology and history at Oxford University for sixteen years and was Dean of Divinity and a fellow of New College, Oxford. She has also served as canon theologian of Salisbury Cathedral and as theological consultant to the Church of England House of Bishops. She is a historian of modern religion; her books include *Miracles in Enlightenment England* (Yale, 2006); *Octavia, Daughter of God: the Story of a Female Messiah and her Followers* (Yale, 2011); and *A Practical Christianity: Meditations for the Season of Lent* (Morehouse, 2012).

George P. Shultz, a graduate of Princeton University and a US Marine Corps veteran, was appointed secretary of labor in 1969, director of the Office of Management and Budget in 1970, and secretary of the treasury in 1972. He served in the Reagan administration as chairman of the President's Economic Policy Advisory Board (1981–82) and secretary of state (1982–89). Since 1989, he has been a distinguished fellow at Stanford University's Hoover Institution. In 2001, he became the Thomas W. and Susan B. Ford Distinguished Fellow. He is honorary chairman of the Stanford Institute for Economic Policy Research Advisory Council and is chair of the Precourt Institute Energy Advisory Council at Stanford, the MIT Energy Initiative External Advisory Board, and the Shultz-Stephenson Task Force on Energy Policy at the Hoover Institution. His publications include *Turmoil and Triumph: My Years as Secretary of State* (1993), *Issues on My Mind: Strategies for the Future* (2013), and *Game Changers: Energy on the Move* (2014).

Christopher William Stubbs is a professor of physics and of astronomy at Harvard University. He is also an Annenberg Distinguished Visiting Fellow at the Hoover Institution. His scientific research interests lie at the intersection of cosmology, particle physics, and gravitation, with more than four hundred publications to date. He also has a strong interest in national security. Stubbs is a member of JASON, a group of scientists and engineers who provide technical advice to government agencies on national security issues. He served on the technical advisory group for the US Senate Select Committee on Intelligence.

William E. Swing, formerly bishop of the Episcopal Diocese of California, is the founder and president of the United Religions Initiative. He has served as a parish priest in West Virginia and Washington, DC, a pioneer of religion's response to the AIDS pandemic, board member of the American Foundation for AIDS research, board chair of the Church Divinity School of the Pacific, chair of numerous diocesan boards, and chair and committee member of numerous boards of the national Episcopal Church, co-chairing joint relations with the Diocese of Jerusalem and then with the Chinese Christian Council. He was instrumental in the founding of a capital development bank in Oakland, California; in the transitioning of St. Luke's Hospital,

San Francisco; in starting San Francisco's largest homeless program; and in rejuvenating and expanding El Rancho del Obispo in Healdsburg, California.

Philip Taubman is a consulting professor at Stanford's Center for International Security and Cooperation, where he is working on the first comprehensive biography of George Shultz. Before joining CISAC in 2008, he worked at the *New York Times* as a reporter and editor for nearly thirty years, specializing in national security issues, including intelligence and defense policies and operations. He serves as secretary of the Stanford University Board of Trustees and is associate vice president for university affairs, working on special projects for Stanford's president, John Hennessy. He is author of *The Partnership: Five Cold Warriors and Their Quest to Ban the Bomb* (Harper Collins, 2012) and *Secret Empire: Eisenhower, the CIA, and the Hidden Story of America's Space Espionage* (Simon & Schuster, 2003).

Tatiana Yankelevich graduated from Moscow University in 1975. As a result of KGB pressure, she emigrated to the United States in 1977, becoming a US citizen in 1983. As an adjunct professor at Bentley College, Waltham, Massachusetts, she taught courses in Russian literature and post-WWII Soviet history. She has been a visiting lecturer at more than thirty American colleges and universities and has delivered lectures and seminars on human rights in Russia. She has maintained Andrei Sakharov's archives and prepared for publication his writings and those of Elena Bonner. From 1993 to 2004, she was assistant director of the Andrei Sakharov Archives at Brandeis University. From 2004 to 2009, she was director of the Sakharov Program on Human Rights at the Davis Center for Russian and Eurasian Studies at Harvard University, now the home of the Andrei Sakharov Archive. She is affiliated with the Davis Center as an independent researcher.

Index